Mockingbird Years

Mockingbird Years

A Life
In and Out
of
Therapy

EMILY FOX GORDON

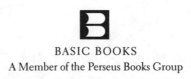

BASIC BOOKS
A Member of the Perseus Books Group

The author wishes to thank the following: The estate of Randall Jarrell for permission to reprint lines from "Well Water" (from *The Lost World*, Macmillan, © 1963).

Martin Buber, *The Knowledge of Man* (St. Leonards, Australia: Allen & Unwin, 1963).

Harcourt, Inc. for permission to reprint an excerpt from "East Coker" in FOUR QUARTETS, copyright 1940 by T. S. Eliot and renewed by Esme Valerie Eliot.

This memoir grew out of material that appeared in the form of the essays "Faculty Brat" (*Boulevard*, Spring 1995, vol. 10, no. 1–2), "Mockingbird Years" (*Boulevard*, Spring 1996, vol. 11, no. 1–2), and "My Last Therapist" (*Salmagundi*, Summer 1999, no. 123).

Published by Basic Books,
A Member of the Perseus Books Group

FIRST PAPERBACK EDITION

Library of Congress Cataloging-in-Publication Data
Gordon, Emily Fox, 1948–
    Mockingbird years : a life in and out of therapy / Emily Fox Gordon.
            p. cm.
    ISBN 0-465-02728-8
    1. Gordon, Emily Fox, 1948– 2. Psychotherapy patients—
United States—Biography. I. Title.
RC464.G67 A3 2000
616.89'14'092—dc21
[B]
99-087907

Designed by Elliott Beard

01 02 03 04 / 10 9 8 7 6 5 4 3 2

For George

CONTENTS

Mockingbird Years

1

RIGGS

When I was eighteen my parents were faced with a problem: what to do with a sullen, disorganized daughter who had failed to graduate high school and who had returned home to Washington, D.C., wrists bandaged, from an extended stay with her boyfriend's mother in Indianapolis. They took me in tow to the psychiatrist I'd been seeing off and on through my high school years, who recommended that I spend some time in a "therapeutic environment." He suggested Austen Riggs, a hospital in Stockbridge, Massachusetts, where patients—none of them too sick, he reassured us—were free to come and go, and where I might spend some months away from the immediate source of my confusion, the boyfriend and his mother.

I stayed at Riggs for three years, one as an inpatient, two as an outpatient, living in apartments with various roommates. These were years I should have been in college, and they were so empty and aimless that when I remember Riggs now, my mind pans around the corridors of the big comfortable patient residence, the

Inn, as we called it, and in my imagination it is absolutely unin-
habited. I drift through the central hall and into the dining room,
where the fruit bowl and the iced tea urn rested on a polished
sideboard, replenished by the staff at regular intervals. I cross the
hall to the living room with its twelve couches, grand piano, and
tall windows hung with flowered chintz curtains. Then I with-
draw to the wide central hall and approach the reception desk
below the great curving central staircase, and wander in memory
through the back door to the grounds, where deck chairs were
arrayed in pairs under the trees. I skim by the volleyball and tennis
courts and across the parking lot behind the medical building,
where patients met with therapists, past the patient-run, staff-
supervised nursery school and the greenhouse.

Riggs was an anachronistic institution even then. (I often wonder what it's like there now; the patients are a lot sicker, I'm told, and
they stay for shorter periods of time.) The population was very
young, very bored. A few middle-aged people were there, but we
younger ones tended to avoid them. They looked baggy and
defeated, truly sad in a way we sensed had more to do with life than
diagnostic categories. Years later, when I actually went to college, I
read The Magic Mountain in a seminar, and I felt I had a certain
advantage over the other students. How well my Riggs experience
prepared me to understand the convalescent languors of the tuber-
culosis patients, reclining on their deck chairs, blankets draped over
their knees, eyes fixed on the middle distance. Now, whenever I see
one of those chairs, the white-painted wooden Adirondack type that
seem to show up in soft-focus lithographs on the walls of so many
doctors' offices, I feel a familiar jelly-limbed ennui.

My suicidal gesture had been feeble, a few swipes with a pair
of nail scissors. I knew when I arrived at Riggs that I was quite sane

and only mildly sick; I had no business being there. But I had no business anywhere else either—no diploma, no prospects, and no ambitions.

I arrived excited; going to Riggs was the fulfillment of an adolescent fantasy. The status of mental patient would invest me with significance. The frantic little act that landed me there had been my entrée to a process; life would work on me in this particularly colorful way, and who knew what might happen? Riggs had a special interest for me because by coincidence I had spent some time hanging around there at age fifteen, when I visited the home of my friend Caroline, whose father was the financial manager of the institution. We had seen the movie *David and Lisa*, a tearjerker about a love affair between two adolescent mental patients, and we were smitten with the romance of madness. I think we believed that if we cultivated dissociation we would become as beautiful as Lisa: Our complexions would turn luminous, our faces grow expressive hollows, our hair lie flat and glossy. We spent our days edging cautiously around the grounds, taking drags on shared cigarettes and muttering "a touch can kill," hoping to be noticed by the patients, drawn into their glamorous orbit by the magic of proximity. The patients frustrated us by staying indoors, their windows open to the July breezes, playing "Mockingbird" on their stereos. We heard this song constantly, from multiple windows under which we passed, and for us its refrain became the perverse anthem of mental illness:

Mock, yeah!
Ing, yeah!
Bird, yeah!
Yeah, yeah!
Mock-ing-bird!

When the psychiatrist in Washington recommended that I be sent to Riggs, I quivered inwardly, afraid to blow it all by showing my pleasure, and the moment I got home and free of my parents I called Caroline long-distance." Guess what?" I whispered. "Guess where I'm going?" Caroline was going to college, but I was going to Riggs, and I knew by the envy in her voice that I had double-trumped her.

At community meetings patients sat cross-legged on couches, or lay sprawled on the carpet, and were encouraged to ventilate their feelings by the nurses and a small, round-eyed man named Richard, a nondoctor whose function I couldn't understand at first, a kind of professional gadfly and controversialist. Years later I found a category for him; he was a protofacilitator, perhaps the first of his kind to emerge from the fledgling family-systems school of psychiatry.

These meetings, meals, and therapy sessions were the only real structure of our days. We were assigned tasks, called "work-jobs," in the mornings, but most patients slept through the hour reserved for them. It felt a little gratuitous to spend an hour sponging down baseboards when that hour was being charged to one's account. The issues of work-jobs and DNR, or day-night reversal (this was the late 1960s, and already we were using acronyms—Riggs was both anachronistic and ahead of its time) were the staples of discussion at community meetings—not so much discussion, really, as nagging and resistance. The nurses and the protofacilitator kept after us. Why couldn't we take pride in our environment? Could we get to the bottom of this, please? The patients sank deeper into silence and into the contorted positions young bodies assume in shamed repose.

The essential passivity of life at Riggs, a life lived to be examined in therapy, worked against the staff's attempts to get us to clean up after ourselves and keep sensible hours. The domestic staff in the Inn—the nurses, the aides, and Richard the protofacilitator—operated at cross-purposes with the therapists, those austere beings in the big white building across the way who received us singly in their offices and were seen in the Inn only when a patient was having what the nurses called an "upset," with the accent on the first syllable of the word, late at night. The therapists viewed our sloth as symptomatic, and we all tacitly understood that any attempt to expunge what was symptomatic in our behavior was antitherapeutic. The therapists were the radicals, the staff the exponents of realpolitik. The conflict between these factions was never open, and perhaps it was never a real one but rather a deliberately engineered tension, a therapeutic master plan, a good-cop, neutral-cop ploy. But even if that was true, I know that like most master plans it was often lost sight of, even by its designers.

Not all of us were normal late adolescents. Some were seriously depressed, not just sluggish. Some were harmlessly odd, like L, a lapsed seminarian who carried on a constant internal debate about the supremacy of the papacy. He would emerge from his room to keep a running score on the blackboard above the mailboxes—L 24, Pope 17. Some of the elderly outpatients seemed beyond hope. The parameters of their worlds shrank as they aged; their compulsiveness stiffened. Never quite accepted by the townspeople, they shuffled up and down Main Street, stopping for the lunch special at the drugstore, ducking into the library for a nap.

A few patients were mad. I recall two in the early days of my stay there; one somehow got her hands on an antique cannon, fiddled with it to make it operational, and fired it out her bedroom window. She also pulled a gun on her therapist, made him plead for his life. The other, a young man who could have doubled for Charles

Manson, stuffed hard-boiled eggs into his rectum and laid them publicly, dropping his pants and squatting in the hallway.

Still, making allowance for the effects of idleness and boredom, I think most Riggs patients were much like people in the outside world. Graduate students, for example, don't seem much saner as a group, or even much happier. The striking difference between Riggs patients and comparable young people living outside was that Riggs patients were richer. I believe I came from the least wealthy family of any patient while I was there.

My mother delivered me to Riggs. She spent the first night with me in the local guest house. We were shown into our room, with its flounced twin beds and space heater, its view of Stockbridge's famous Main Street, the one painted by Norman Rockwell. She closed the door and took her flask from her purse. "I guess the sun's over the yardarm," she said.

The next morning was frosty and bright; we said our farewells in the parking lot of the therapy building, and she alarmed me by bursting into tears, very uncharacteristic behavior. "Goodbye, my dear," she said, and clutched me. The sun bounced off the lenses of her dark glasses and blazed in car windshields. I remember staring over her shoulder blankly, eager to see her go, eager to get started.

I was led from office to office in the warren of small rooms in the basement of the therapy building, tested and interviewed by five or six of the psychiatrists on staff. I was given the standard Wechsler intelligence quotient test for adults. (What is the Koran? What does the following quotation mean: "A single swallow does not a summer make?" Assemble these blocks so that the result exactly reproduces the pattern in this booklet. Tell me a story that explains this picture—a boy stands at the head of the stairs, a broken violin in his hand. A man stands over him.) I was given a Rorschach, a personality inventory. When I hesitated, the examiner leaned back in his chair, drummed the desk with his thumbs, took a furtive look at his stopwatch. "Take your time," he said.

When my diagnostic workup was complete, I became the subject of a full-dress staff conference in which my prognosis was discussed and my treatment plan drawn up. I think I may have been the last patient at Riggs to be brought into her own conference. The custom was dropped, probably because it had an unenlightened, nineteenth-century feel about it.

I remember entering that room, led in by a nurse, shown to a chair at the head of a polished oval table that seemed to me the size of a fishing boat. The nurse withdrew. Seated there, looking down the rows of faces that looked back inquiringly into mine, I was visited with an impulse to say, "Perhaps you gentlemen were wondering why I called you all together today." That made me smirk inappropriately. "Emily," said one of the doctors, "I'm interested in this detached feeling you described in your interview—that floating, disengaged sensation. Are you feeling that way right now?"

"I guess I am," I said, and I lifted my lowered eyes to hazard a smile at the assembled doctors. They smiled back encouragingly, and at that moment I felt a desolate certainty that now there would be no backing out. Now I had left home for good.

I was a hog for attention and welcomed nearly any kind, but the doctors' questions, the nurses' charting of my moods and actions, all this had the feel of the speculum about it.

Within a few months, though, the staff's vigilance had dissipated, and I took my place among the other patients, lounging on the leather sofas in the entrance hall, ashtray balanced on my knee, running my eyes over back issues of *Horizon*. I learned to scorn the activities Riggs offered, ceramics and woodworking in the shop, repotting plants in the greenhouse. I learned to pretend that I hated the food, which was actually the best institutional food I had ever eaten or ever have since. My adjustment was quick and unproblematic.

I was assigned to a therapist, a research psychologist. I learned later that I was only his second clinical patient. He was a man in his middle thirties, amiable, earnest, eager. He had a spade-shaped, high-cheekboned, luminous face—a beautiful face, really—that sat at an odd angle to his neck, a disc facing up rather than out, and he stood rocked forward on his toes, his shoulders so hunched they were nearly level with his ears. My adolescent sensors instantly registered something alien and slightly goony in his aspect, and I never fully accepted him. Now I understand him better; experience has provided me with a context into which I can place him. He came from the Bronx, a *yeshiva bucher* from a Yiddish-speaking household. When I think of him now, I put a yarmulke on his balding head and append Hassidic curls to his temples, and I see his face as a throwback to visionary and ecstatic ancestors.

I was retested a year after I arrived, and my IQ had declined significantly—how much, my therapist wouldn't tell me. He would only say the test results were "disappointing." My diagnosis was altered. Now my anxiety neurosis had become a "schizoid personality disorder with borderline trends." This is a bad diagnosis, and an insulting one, I've been told since, but at the time I rather liked the sound of "borderline trends." It made me think of a stylish flourish, an extra, like piping on a jacket or whitewall tires on a car.

Apathy wasted us. I had been a failure as a student, but I had always read voraciously. At Riggs I stopped. We lost our normal adolescent interest in sex—for the most part, at least. We hung out in groups, but we tended not to form real friendships; we saw one another as fundamentally inaccessible, three-quarters submerged. We wore kimonos and hair curlers, jeans and slippers, as we padded around the Inn—half dressed, half there. News of the Vietnam War protests reached us; we crowded into the patient library where the record player was kept to listen to *Blonde on Blonde, Music from Big Pink,* and *Abbey Road,* but still we felt wistfully peripheral. The great countercultural storm was rising but far away from us. Actually, to the degree that a therapeutic view of life has been a legacy of the 1960s, we seem in retrospect to have been an advance guard. But at the time we viewed ourselves as the last of the stragglers.

Many of us got worse rather than better, and for some, getting worse was dangerous. By the time some patients ran out of money, and this was bound to happen eventually, even to the multimillion-dollar trust-funders, their parents and doctors had come to view them as too debilitated to go back into the world. Instead they moved on to state institutions, where sometimes they stayed for life.

Toward the end of my first year as a Riggs patient, my therapist became inappropriately attached to me. Our meetings were charged with feeling, and every session seemed to end in an epiphany. But it was Dr. S's eyes that beaded with tears, not mine. My parents, we acknowledged in therapy, had rejected and abandoned me. I had known this for years, but pretended it was a revelation because I found his emotion too gratifying not to play on. At the same time, I felt itchy and uncomfortable, instantly sated with his love, made queasy by it. I'm not sure whether this was because I felt myself to be in bad faith or whether I was unaccustomed to this kind of moony empathy, this cherishing pity. I was not the kind of young girl a lot of men fell in love with. And I always felt that the object of

Dr. S's love was not me but some phantasmal waif who only half inhabited the chair in which I sat.

"Thank you," I would say as we paused at the door of his office at the end of an hour. "No, thank *you*," Dr. S said. I had opened up the world of feeling for him, he told me. The years of charts and statistics and rat mazes were over for him now. We began to take walks on autumn days. Dr. S taught me to drive and accompanied me when I took my driving test. I taught him to smoke cigarettes.

Around the time Dr. S's wife was due to deliver a baby, I became an outpatient. Dr. S began to appear at my door. One evening we drank a lot of wine, he and my roommate and I, and we all took a tipsy walk after dinner. Dr. S put his arm around my waist. This was the first physical contact between us, and the only, but it changed things unalterably. I woke the next morning charged with a theatrical anger and teased by doubts about its legitimacy.

In therapy I remained mostly silent after this incident, and glared. Dr. S became frantic. He told me one day that he had spent the morning weeping in his parked car on a farm road in Lenox, one of the routes we often took on our drives. Hearing this confession puffed me up with scorn like a blowfish. I was thrilled and enraged. Inwardly, I felt some alarm at this reaction; it seemed partly out of my control. My disgust at Dr. S had something to do with the way his clammy feelings for me entwined with professional ambition — at my second staff conference he presented our work together as a new way of doing therapy in which the therapist makes himself vulnerable, fully embraces his own transference, drops his therapeutic distance. A triumph, except for my unfortunate deterioration, documented in testing. But that was easily finessed with the familiar psychoanalytic rationalization that explains an increase in symptoms as a necessary precursor to a breakthrough. As for my baleful new diagnosis, that was drawn from the testing. Having forsworn objectivity in his dealings with me, Dr. S took no part in it.

I was witnessing the final collapse of adult authority, and my anger was a cover for fear. But it also served to conceal a kind of sexual frustration. I think my semiconscious thought process went something like this: If I'm going to do something so extreme and destructive as to have an affair with my married therapist, I want him to be so powerful, so seductive, that my culpability is washed away. I want his passion to overwhelm me and leave me blameless. But Dr. S's feeling for me was more emotional than sexual, more tender than passionate. I could feel a smug slackness in the arm that encircled my waist, tentativeness in his dangling fingers as they brushed against my hip, and it made me mad. I never fully acknowledged this to myself at the time. But let me give my former self the highly qualified credit she deserves; my self-suspicion was like a thready, persistent extra pulse.

I began an unsystematic search for a new therapist, approaching doctors who looked sympathetic and explaining guardedly that I felt I would do better with somebody more experienced than Dr. S. The answer was always the same: This is an issue to be worked out in therapy.

The new director arrived, startling us all with his appearance. He was tall and bony, with a comic villain's brilliantined black hair and a waist that seemed to begin six inches below his lantern jaw. He wore cowboy boots and string ties, and he brought with him a bevy of beautiful psychotic young girls from the hospital he had directed in Washington, D.C. He was a swashbuckler, a florid, impulsive personality, famous for his hands-on treatment: If the patient crawled under a bed, the story went, he crawled under too and conducted the session right there.

But those girls! They were like a team of NBA all-stars trooping in to watch a junior college practice. They quickly showed us their tricks: One inserted needles in the pupils of her eyes; another plastered her face with chalky makeup and walked around the Inn with her eyes closed and arms extended, a Kabuki somnambulist. A third became a member of my therapy group (Subgroup C), and she enlivened the proceedings by screaming at unpredictable intervals, full-throated operatic screams that lasted for fifteen seconds. The arrival of these girls precipitated an avalanche of competitive upsets among the patients, and the nurses had their hands full for a few months. Then these patients, too, "settled in," being human as well as mad.

Dr. Leslie Farber came to Riggs with the new administration. He was an old friend of the director, who lured him with promises of time to spend on his writing. I first saw him when he visited our community meeting, which began with the usual nagging by the nurses and Richard about the work-jobs left undone, the unwholesome hour at which most of the inpatients had gone to bed, followed by the usual silence and then the dribble of patient complaints. Sue M, the lanky Floridian, wanted to know why scrambled eggs could not be substituted for the food offered at every meal, not just breakfast. Howard Z, a new patient housed in the east wing of the Inn, complained that trucks making early morning deliveries to the kitchen were waking him.

Diana D spoke next, from her cross-legged position on the floor, leaning forward from the waist, arching her neck and gesturing extravagantly. Diana's speaking style was expressive and tormented. She would make a stab at saying something, fail, erase the air with flailing palms, cover her face with her hands and rock back and forth on her haunches, then try again. Today she said: "I . . . I don't feel very good about this, but I'm just so uncomfortable. I don't think this is something I can say."

"We're listening, Diana," said Richard. "We want to hear what you have to say."

Diana hesitated. "It's the outpatients," she said. "The outpatients are making me depressed. Especially John Haviland. I wish he didn't have to come into the Inn. I wish he didn't have to eat with us. He's so depressing, the way he eats." John Haviland, wearing a soiled windbreaker, looked up from the piano bench by the window. He was a little man with a built-up shoe. He was often the object of imitations by the late-night crew in the patient kitchen; stuffing a roll of toilet paper down the front of one's pants and locking one knee helped to evoke his off-center lumpiness and his fractured gait. "When they're around, the older ones, I feel like that's how I'm going to end up, and I don't want to have to look at that. I don't really think I should have to."

I had been stealing looks at Dr. Farber, who sat quietly in the wing chair by the fireplace. I had noted that he was slightly plump, balding, and middle-aged, with an elfin-Semitic face and an air of masculine elegance that none of his constituent physical parts accounted for. (Later I learned from him how he felt about his embodiment: "a fat little Jewish dentist," he said, quoting a former patient.) In the silence after Diana's remarks, I slid my eyes in his direction again and saw on his face an unmistakable expression of shocked contempt. His eyebrows were arched, his lip curled, his nostrils distended.

This look jolted me. I knew instantly that Dr. Farber was a different kind of being from the other therapists. His was not the neutral watchfulness I had become so used to; he judged, and revealed his judgment. This was striking enough, but it was really just the first layer of my reaction. I also sensed, if obscurely, that he was a person whose way of looking at the world—unlike that of any therapist I had encountered—was integrated with, and undetachable from, his self.

I learned later that Dr. Farber was well known not only in psychoanalytic circles but in the wider intellectual world as well. He was a maverick, humane and cultivated, who challenged his colleagues to confront what the science of psychology had refused to acknowledge—the inextinguishable presence of will in human behavior.

In one of his essays Dr. Farber compared the psychoanalyst to Kierkegaard's "systematizer," a man who has spent decades building a splendid mansion, a great multistoried edifice with wings flung out in every direction. But when the man has finally completed his dream house, he settles contentedly into a shack next door. In Dr. Farber's view, the house of psychoanalysis was impressive but unfit for human habitation.

Dr. Farber's face, its expression that afternoon, was a life lesson for me, the first I had received since I willingly immured myself at Riggs, a very dense, impacted lesson that I would spend years absorbing and have yet to learn completely.

I made an appointment with Dr. Farber immediately, and once seated in his office I wasted no time in blurting out the story of Dr. S and the driving lessons and the baby Mrs. S had just given birth to and the arm around my waist and his tears. I felt some terror as I spoke; Dr. Farber's dour expression was not encouraging. He heard me out without interruption, though, and when I was finished he agreed it would be impossible for me to continue in therapy with Dr. S. Which doctors on the staff would I consider compatible? I didn't really know, I said. They seemed kind of indistinguishable from one another. Would he, Dr. Farber, take me on as a patient? No, he said; his docket was already full. We sat in silence for a few minutes.

Next Dr. Farber startled me by asking what I thought of Washington, D.C. He had just come from there, he said, and he had noticed a Washington address in my file. I stalled, floundered. What could this question mean? Finally I said that I liked Washington, although it was kind of a weird city. He nodded gravely. It *is* kind of weird, and I like it too, he said. He added that he was having some trouble adjusting to Stockbridge. Did anybody actually work around here, or were the townspeople all models for Norman Rockwell? I laughed explosively. A joke!

We went on to talk about other subjects. Poetry: Did I like John Crowe Ransom, a special enthusiasm of his? Yes, I did, I replied, although I had never read or heard of John Crowe Ransom. Dr. Farber stubbed out his Camel and propelled himself headlong out of his chair so abruptly that for a moment I feared he was having a seizure. He rummaged in one of the cardboard boxes that surrounded his desk—he was still unpacking his library—and drew out a book. He tossed it to me, and I caught it two-handed. Take it, he said. You can return it when you come back to talk to me next week. He moved to the door and opened it. What about therapy? I asked, rising from my seat. Do without therapy for a while, he said, ushering me out. Just come back next week and we'll talk.

My father was understandably outraged when he learned that I had gone without therapy for three weeks. Just talking, he shouted over the phone, at eighty dollars a day? Just chatting? He handed the receiver to my mother.

I read the Ransom anxiously, preparing myself to be quizzed, but when I awkwardly rose from my chair in Dr. Farber's office to hand back the book—even the simplest physical transactions between patient and therapist made me self-conscious—Dr. Farber took it, opened and leafed through it, reading passages aloud in his fine deep voice, smiling, shaking his head in confounded admiration. "The curse of hell upon the sleek upstart," he read,

> That got the Captain finally on his back
> And took the red red vitals of his heart
> And made the kites to whet their beaks clack clack.

(I copy these lines from the same Vintage paperback Dr. Farber threw at me more than thirty years ago, one of many books he lent me and that I never returned.) Involuntarily, in a burst of delight, I clapped my hands and repeated "clack clack." I blushed. Dr. Farber smiled his odd, wounded smile, and we lapsed into a long, for me unnerving, appreciative silence.

I was desperately eager to please Dr. Farber, but the open-endedness of our arrangement made me so anxious that my conversational timing was thrown off. I sensed that he was wavering in his refusal to accept me as a patient, that I was being auditioned, and the more urgently I wished to pass this obscure test, the more clumsy and aggressive my efforts to win him became. Too shy and fearful of rejection to plead, I sometimes veered off into truculence, imposed my own attention-demanding silences. I wanted to talk about Dr. S, my parents, myself. So we talked about these things, but in a novel kind of way. I told him the particulars of the mess that had precipitated my suicidal gesture—the boyfriend and his mother, the train ride from Indianapolis to Washington when I lay in a roomette and wept myself sick. And instead of inviting me to continue with a receptively neutral psychoanalytic silence, he forthrightly responded with an anecdote from his own life. He told me about the breakup of his first marriage, the car trip he took from San Francisco to New York, driving for eighteen hours a day and collapsing in roadside motels for six. I hung on these stories, these amazing offerings, but when they ended I lapsed into panic. What now? How was I to respond? And could any response be adequate? I wanted to lift Dr. Farber's confidences out of the hour, out of their contextual bedding, and take them home with me to gnaw on in private, extract all the nourishment to be had from them.

Did I like Joanne Woodward? This one came from far left field. Did I? I asked myself, and rummaged frantically in the underused opinion-forming sector of my mind. Finding no ready-made response, I asked myself what movies I had seen in which Joanne Woodward appeared. I knew I'd seen some, but my memory was clouded and roiled with anxiety. I called up an image of Joanne Woodward's face. Yes, I said. It's her face I like. It's plain and handsome at the same time. It's very direct. Yes, said Dr. Farber, with gratifying emphasis. That's the thing about her, all right. And we went on to talk about Joanne Woodward movies, a few of which, now that I had relaxed, bobbed up naturally onto the surface of my recollection.

Thus does the despairer appear before us to ask that most extraordinary and truly diabolical question—especially when addressed to a psychotherapist—"is there any good in talking?" After this, we may recover our composure and succeed in engaging him imaginatively, so that real talk does, after all, begin to come about. Despite his absolute certainty of a few moments before that even momentary relief from the torment of despair was no longer possible, his despairing self-absorption may yield to forthright interest in the subject at hand, a yielding which goes beyond mere distraction. Relief has, in spite of everything, actually been granted him; his despairing certainty has been exposed to the real world of discourse and proved false. We might even say that a minor miracle has occurred. What are we to answer then, when, as the hour nears its end, our patient or friend, preparing to take his leave, turns to us and asks, "But haven't you something *useful* to say to me—something I can use after I leave here?" If there is an answer to this question, it has not occurred to me.

This passage comes from Dr. Farber's essay "Despair and the Life of Suicide," and it describes exactly the experience of therapy— or friendship; for him the two were inseparable—with Dr. Farber. "The real world of discourse"—this is where we are all free to live when we live outside of systems, but I had lived inside one for a long time. Years of psychotherapy had made me smoothly practiced at collapsing into my components, exposing them for convenient inspection on cue. I had learned to "assume the position" so automatically that Dr. Farber's requirement that I come to our talks as pulled together as possible—ready to exercise judgment, to make distinctions, to listen and respond, to view myself first as a moral and then a psychological being, most important, to tell the truth; to accept the high value he placed on tact, empathy, intellectual substance, wit—all this bewildered me at first. It bewildered me later too. In fact, it bewilders me now all over again, having lived for nearly twenty years after Dr. Farber's death in a culture that has become saturated with therapy, in a world that has become a hospital.

The patient or friend in this passage is in despair, for Dr. Farber a very specific state, which he vividly describes and carefully documents as a drastic spiritual condition that presents its sufferer with an opportunity for redemption at the same time that it provides "fertile soil" for the "intrigues" of suicide." What bothers me when I read this passage is a nagging sense that, at least while I was a patient at Riggs, I never was the patient or friend of whom Dr. Farber speaks here. "[D]espair seems to afflict only those whose relation to life is a serious and potentially responsible one," he remarks later in his essay. I hope I was "potentially responsible," but I don't believe I was "serious" in the way Dr. Farber's hypothetical friend was serious. Despair was not my condition; neediness was. In fact, from my perspective now, in middle age, the story of my attachment to Dr. Farber would seem drawn more likely from the annals of primatology than from philosophy or theology (the latter was Dr. Farber's real stomping ground). It seems plain to me now that while I felt the purest and most ardent admiration for him that I had ever felt for anybody, I was also an unprotected young female trying to find refuge in the care of a "silverback," a dominant male.

Dr. Farber was extremely sedentary; his idea of exercise was to fumble energetically for his lighter when it fell between the cushions of his red leather chair. Now that he and his family had moved to the country, his wife persuaded him to buy a bike and ride it to Riggs in the morning. He fell off the bicycle almost immediately, cracked a rib and broke an arm.

He sat uncomfortably upright, twisted to shield his injured right side from collisions with the arm of his chair, lighting his innumerable cigarettes one-handedly. He looked miserable. After a few minutes of halting monologue, I reverted to the politeness I had been taught in early childhood and suggested he go home. He thanked me, and we broke off the session.

The next week he greeted me with warmth. His arm was still in a sling, but he looked much better. At the end of the hour he announced almost casually that a space had opened up and he would, after all, be able to take me on as a patient.

Dr. Farber insisted that I have a final, civil talk with Dr. S. I protested that I was too angry at Dr. S to speak to him. Dr. Farber suggested that I consider the connection between guilt and anger. I countered with genuine indignation that Dr. S was far more guilty than I. Dr. Farber allowed that, and observed that the greater guilt did not completely mitigate the lesser. I made the appointment and spent an hour with Dr. S. I think he cried, and I do remember walking into his office with the sullen air of a child forced by adults to apologize. Now I want to say to my former self: You didn't need to apologize, you dolt! You needed to ask to see the baby pictures, and to say good-bye.

I had come to view guilt as a noxious psychic by-product, something to be gotten rid of in the interest of health. It took me a while to grasp that Dr. Farber's idea was different: For him guilt was real. It was a moral state rather than a psychological condition.

Dr. Farber's attitude toward me was never the "unconditional positive regard" with which therapists are charged to view their patients. His regard was highly qualified and partial, and it was as real as rock.

*   *   *

I studied for and passed my GED certification. I took a few night classes at the local community college. I began to read again, mostly books lent to me by Dr. Farber—Goncharov's *Oblomov* (appropriate for me), Martin Buber's *I and Thou*, which I still fail to appreciate, poems by Randall Jarrell and Phillip Larkin. I got a summer job in the kitchen of a summer camp. "Girl, we've got to teach you to *work*," said the cook, and I quit after a few weeks.

I also began to get myself in trouble with alcohol and bad companions. When night fell we could be found at the Stockbridge Inn, known to regulars as Simmy's, drinking beer and waiting to be picked up. Simmy's was full of local characters, pool-players laid off from their jobs at G.E., reprobates thrown out of their houses by their wives, glumly stewing at the bar, low-life freeriders on the sexual revolution, buying us drinks and dragging a *carpe diem* line.

I became promiscuous, and I confessed my promiscuity to Dr. Farber. I think I told him about every encounter. His response was surprisingly muted. Again? he would say. Once he called me a "female jerk." He got truly angry only when the man in question was married.

Why did I behave that way? I can think of psychoanalytic explanations: Perhaps I was "acting out" the unconscious feelings that Dr. S's seductiveness had aroused in me, or, more likely, punishing myself for having rejected him and having won Dr. Farber as a protector. I can think of obvious explanations: I was bored, and getting picked up was fun.

I tried out my hypotheses on Dr. Farber. His response was to cut me off. "I'm not interested in that," he would say. His approach, as always, seemed to steer a slalom course around the causal markers I had put in place. Instead he turned the discussion to my drinking and to drinking in general. We talked about the coarsening of feeling, the blurring of distinctions, and the deadening of thought that habitual drunkenness brings about. He also talked about the joy of another kind of nonhabituated drinking. Stop the bad kind of drinking, he advised me, so that you can regain the good kind. You were meant, he told me during one of those talks, for the conscious life.

I carry that around with me still, and also the "female jerk" remark. One negative, one positive—both were his gifts of confirmation.

Then I got pregnant, not by one of my Simmy's pickups but as a result of a brief re-encounter with another patient who had been my boyfriend for a summer.

I had skipped a period, felt sick in the mornings, but I refused to acknowledge my condition until one of the nurses, a local woman with a pungent sense of humor, whacked me on the rear as I stood serving myself in the Riggs dining room and made a remark about eating for two. Then I panicked.

A Pittsfield gynecologist confirmed my condition. There are certain circumstances in which bringing a pregnancy to term may not be advisable, he told me. Do what you can do on your own, and call me in two weeks if you haven't had any luck. Perhaps they can help you at Riggs. I wonder now why I didn't take this as a veiled and provisional assurance that he would give me an abortion (then illegal). That was surely what he meant. Instead, I put emphasis on his instruction to "do what I could."

When Dr. Farber asked me if I wanted my parents told, I said *no*. I did tell two of my inpatient friends about the pregnancy, though, and soon everybody knew. The director barged into Dr. Farber's office and demanded that my parents be called immediately. The institution would be liable, he insisted, for anything that happened to me. He picked up the phone receiver. Dr. Farber snatched it away, as he later told me, and a physical struggle ensued. The image of a wrestling match between that aging Mutt and Jeff pair seems hilarious to me now, and Dr. Farber's part in it heroic.

Dr. Farber reported to me that the director had suggested a therapeutic abortion. This would require Dr. Farber's assent and his signature on a document attesting to my unfitness to bear and raise a child. Dr. Farber explained his refusal carefully; he could not arrange the abortion because he could not agree with such a statement. I nodded, barely listening. He had raised my hopes and dashed them, but I felt no resentment, no reaction except an acceleration of panic.

I spent a week on the phone, following leads, being scolded long-distance by abortion activists for my past failure to get involved in the issue. Finally I was instructed to dial a New York number, to wait until the phone was picked up and to give my number and area code to the silent person at the end of the line, then to wait for a call. I followed these instructions; the phone rang and a deep, emphysematous male voice told me to be at the Port Authority bus terminal at a certain date and time the following week, standing next to the third phone booth at the Forty-second Street entrance. I was to bring six hundred dollars in cash.

I got the money from the ex-boyfriend, and the two friends in whom I had confided drove me to New York. I waited at the designated place until I was approached by a little man in a green suede cap, who beckoned me out of the terminal and into the back of a limousine, where I was soon joined by an engaged couple from Teaneck, New Jersey. We were all blindfolded and driven to some place in the Bronx (my friends, I learned later, were following in their car). I waited in the parked limousine while the couple was ushered into a building. They emerged a half hour later, the girl walking a little unsteadily, the boy shielding her solicitously with his arm.

Then it was my turn to follow the little man up the back stairs, to shake hands solemnly with "Dr. Adams," to lie down on my back on a linoleum table in a kitchen furnished as sparely as a stage set while five or six radios blared, all tuned to different stations, a crude wall of sound. It was over soon, and I was given pads and an envelope full of antibiotics and allowed to go.

I was delighted to see my friends waiting for me at the end of the block, waving and jumping. They had spent the time eating a late lunch at a nearby Chinese restaurant, and they had saved me an eggroll.

Later that evening I stood dialing Dr. Farber's Stockbridge number, up to my wobbly ankles in sawdust in the back of a West Village bar and steakhouse, full of brandy alexanders and Demerol. Dr. Farber's wife answered and handed the phone immediately to Dr. Farber. "You're all right?" he said. I heard his wife whisper "Thank God!" in the background. Years later, when I got to know her well, she told me that Dr. Farber had spent hours that day in acute anxiety, pacing back and forth in his study.

I launched into a description of my experience, but he cut me off. "Tell me later. You really feel all right?" I feel *fine*, I said, and I did. I was celebrating my passage through a rite; my friends were treating me with respect and solicitude; the adventure had ended safely and I was high as a kite. At the end of the conversation I said something like "You're really a great guy!" or perhaps "I love you!" I don't remember.

*   *   *

Many of the things Dr. Farber said have acted on me much later with a "time-release" effect. It was many years after his death when I finally understood his refusal to endorse a therapeutic abortion for me. At the time I had dismissed it, if I thought about it at all, as adult boilerplate, the kind of carefully worded refusal every adolescent recognizes. Now I realized *he really meant it.* He did not refuse to sign this statement because of a legalistic moral scrupulousness; he refused because he believed I was able, even then, to bear and raise a child.

I'm retrospectively relieved that I had an abortion. I cannot imagine myself in one of my many chaotic apartments, feeding and rocking and changing a baby. Apparently Dr. Farber could, though, and perhaps he was right. But whether or not he was right doesn't matter; what does is his faith in me, which took me more than twenty years to appreciate, or perhaps to accept.

Was Dr. Farber acting out of an antiabortion agenda? He was, after all, a religious man, a private and nonobservant but passionate believer. Was his refusal to endorse a therapeutic abortion an attempt to influence me? No. He was an anti-ideologue and no manipulator. He took the crisis of my pregnancy far more seriously than I did; he understood it as a true dilemma, and he showed a respect for me that I perhaps did not deserve by allowing it to be mine.

Have I found myself, now that I am older and the mother of a living child, capable of guilt about that abortion? Not really. I find I can't advance very far along the path of speculation about alternative fates for that dead fetus without backing up in confusion. The voice of the conceptus is too faint, too garbled and muted by the distance of time and the crosscutting static of possibility for me to hear it clearly. He is no more apparent to me than Dr. Farber's God.

I am just as needy now as I was then. But perhaps by now I've also become the serious friend—the person capable of despair—of whom Dr. Farber wrote. This is the question that continues to haunt me: What would Dr. Farber make of me now? How would he judge the person I've become?

2

BEFORE THERAPY

I am one of those people—we're not so very rare—for whom life has been not so much examined as conducted in therapy. In the place of a conventional moral and cultural education, I was offered therapy, and when the beguiling emptiness of therapy left me hungry for something like spiritual nourishment, I was offered still more therapy. I was formed by therapy, absorbing its influence in ways that would require most of my life to raise to consciousness. I brought into my therapies not the problems of life but the problems of therapy. Even the glowingly subversive moral lessons of Dr. Farber came to me under the cloak of therapy.

But there was a time when my life was innocent of therapy; this was exactly the time, of course, when the unmined and unexamined materials of therapy lay scattered all around me, glittering like geodes.

I recently went looking through a box of old photographs and found a series of my mother with my brother and me in Williamstown, Massachusetts, where I spent my first ten years. These small, curled, black-and-white snapshots were taken in the late 1940s and early 1950s, and they are marked by the pathos and authority of a different time. In one of them my mother stands in the yard of our first house, in front of the hydrangea bushes; their bright blue berries are a radioactive grayish white in the picture. In the background I can see one side of the Williams College library and the marble pediment that ran below its roof, emblazoned with the names OVID, HORACE, EUCLID, and PLATO. My mother holds my brother, Andy, still an infant, in her arms. She is wearing a wool coat that my sister remembers as orange, and I fail to remember at all, with a heavy cowl collar. I stand at my mother's side, age two, wearing overalls and tam-o'-shanter. My sister, five years my senior, is absent from the picture, as she is from all the photographs in this batch, though not from the many scrapbooks that record her infancy.

My father, presumably, is behind the camera. Or perhaps a neighbor is taking the picture and my father is seated at his desk in his study behind the gabled window in the picture, stuffing one kitchen match after another into the bowl of his pipe in an effort to light it, or toting a briefcase full of blue books up the stairs of Furnald Hall, the small white clapboard building across the street where the offices of the Williams economics department were housed, or talking shop with a colleague in the library stacks.

It's my mother's face I'm looking for—the squinting, diamond-shaped eyes, the delicately molded retroussé nose, the long upper lip and the twisting, rueful mouth. Looking at the picture, I can remember it in all its mobility, but I know that the moment I put away the photograph, my mother's face will revert to an empty oval in my mind. I can picture later stages of her face quite adequately; I remember it in early middle age, during the Washington years, when everyone remarked on how, in profile, she looked exactly like a feminized version of John F. Kennedy. I remember her face later, in her fifties and sixties, when it grew pouchy and dejected. A few months before her death, her face began to light up intermittently, sometimes brilliantly; as she bantered with the interns, I saw flashes of the charming girl she had been before I knew her.

In my early childhood, my mother was a significant blur to me. She was multitalented—indifferent to music but a competent pianist, a prolific seamstress, a watercolorist and cartoonist, a brilliant cook, a wit, a teacher with advanced pedagogical notions, an unrealized writer with perfect literary pitch. It seemed to me then that nothing was beyond her powers, but now I believe that being so uniformly good at so many things was a kind of misfortune for my mother. As she perfected her skills, they became smoother and smaller; they became miniature.

She was subject to melancholy. I remember catching a glimpse of her in her sewing room, a length of periwinkle blue corduroy draped across her lap, her mouth full of pins and her eyes full of tears. She spent unexplained and inexplicable idle days at her desk, musing and doodling, drawing women's fingernails, perfectly oval, with delicately shaded quarter-moon cuticles.

Beyond the borders of the photograph lies Williamstown, which I need no prompting to remember, because it sits like a diorama in the center of my memory. Every night as I lower myself into sleep, I run my mind's eye over the town in counterclockwise spiral swaths; my point of origin is the gentle declivity next to the college library where the two houses we occupied, one after the other, sat next to each other. Both were rented from the college—nearly everybody did this at Williams, and the custom had something to do with the charmed quality of life there in the 1950s, the very natural assumption of community among the faculty and their families, the sense that the college was a benign sponsoring presence in their lives, and that nobody ever quite needed to grow up.

Both our houses were rambling wooden ones; the first, which I remember as "the gray house," was a cozy, gabled structure but visually incoherent; it looked as if it had been created by slamming two smaller houses together. That house had the distinction of being seriously considered when scouts went searching for a quintessentially academic setting for the movie *Who's Afraid of Virginia Woolf?*

My brother and I shared a room in the gray house until he was four and I was five. As I study pictures of the two of us clowning in our pajamas, comradely arms thrown around each other's shoulders, I must admit that we were charming little children, goofy and radiant in our delight with one another. Around the time that picture was taken, my mother decided to replace the wallpaper in our room, and we were allowed to draw on it with our crayons. After some parallel scribbling, we came to an agreement to collaborate on a joint project, the depiction of a giant egg with a blurred, man-in-the-moon face. This required planning and cooperation and the use of a chair to stand on. When we had finished—and this is the part of the anecdote that has fascinated many a therapist, so much so that I begin to feel like an old vaudevillian every time I trot it out—we fell onto our knees and worshiped our creation.

The other house was outwardly a conventional Victorian wedding cake; inside it was full of architectural oddities and hiding places. We took it over when it was vacated by the Rudolphs, a tall, Teutonically handsome faculty family, whom my brother and I suspected of being rich. I'm not quite sure why we moved, but I know that the college-sponsored game of domestic musical chairs went on continuously; families changed houses as often as professors changed offices. The chairman of the drama department and his family took our place in the gray house. He and his hard-drinking, glamorously bohemian wife gave raucous parties that spilled out on the lawn. Early one morning Thornton Wilder, there for a production of *Our Town*, woke us by staggering around under our windows, calling "Here kitty, kitty, kitty."

I can retrieve nothing from my childhood as clearly as the wallpaper in the gray house's dining room, red-combed roosters in rectangular broken-lined enclosures. I ran my three-year-old hands along those smooth walls, my eyes tightly shut, muttering, "a rooster, a rooster, a rooster." Another child might have counted the roosters. For me, it was enough to repeat the name, over and over. The second house I remember more comprehensively but less eidetically. I can follow its complex floor plan in my memory, but many of the rooms themselves are blurs or reconstructions. I remember that house mostly for the view out of my attic window; from there I could see College Place snaking around the library, the college buildings and the elms, which even then were moribund and leafless, sketchy goblets filled with air.

My early childhood was one of those idyllic ones that are possible only when beautiful natural surroundings are combined with benign parental neglect. My brother and I understood that my mother had ceded a power of surrogacy to the town. With its summer fields full of wild strawberries and Queen Anne's lace, its semicommunal vegetable gardens, backyard shortcuts, and secret paths through the woods, Williamstown was such a gentle, fostering place that we accepted it as an extension of her.

Sometimes with Andy and sometimes alone, I spent my after-noons rambling around town on my bike. I visited the Haystack Monument, a marble obelisk commemorating a group of pre–World War I Williams students who pledged their lives to missionary work when they took shelter under a haystack on that spot during a thunderstorm. Always a fool for inspiring words, I left my bike lying on the curb, its wheels spinning, while I read the inscription aloud to myself, just as I did the vacuous but fine-sounding exhortation carved into a brass plaque on one of the ivy-covered brick gates of a quadrangle at another end of the campus:

> *Climb High*
> *Climb Far*
> *Your Aim the Sky*
> *Your Goal the Star*

Sometimes I stopped at Lehman Hall, a freshman dormitory where I sought admittance by climbing the fire escape and tapping on windows. My brother, who was more obedient than I, would stay on the ground, clutching the handlebars of his bike and gazing up at me anxiously. Often I got no response to my importunities, or if I did manage to catch a student's attention, I was waved away: Beat it! some young male would mouth through the glass. If I persisted, he might jack open the window and suggest that I come back when I was sixteen. In another mood, he and his roommates would usher me in and feed me chunks of salami cut with a Swiss Army knife, let me sip the foam off their beer, allow me to examine a collection of pornographic playing cards, or toss a softball back and forth with me in the echoing stairwell.

I cruised down to the rural part of the campus, past the tennis courts and the field house and the frog pond. (I notice that as I visualize these places, the images I call up are static and flat and impossible to rotate. When I try to view the pond from a vantage point only slightly less familiar than the standard one, it wavers and stammers like a faulty television picture, and soon it is swallowed up by an encroaching wedge of darkness.) I continued past the small development of red brick row houses that my parents called "Poker Flats," where they had lived before they had children, and where, I gathered, the goings-on had been rakishly semicommunal. I biked along one edge of a big uncut field on the edge of a woods, a half-wild place that, perhaps because of some now-forgotten illustration in one of my schoolbooks, I associated with early American pilgrim life.

I took up the return portion of my ride now, turning right onto Southworth Street, where the houses were slightly narrower and closer together, primmer versions of the big unkempt Victorians where senior faculty lived. My parents had occupied the top floor of a house here when my sister was a baby. Southworth was the boundary between the college part of the town and the "townie" part. Beyond it the streets were laid out in a grid, and the houses were small and boxy, some painted the Easter-egg colors of genteel poverty.

I rode past the yellow funeral home, with its grimly overmanicured square of unnaturally bright green lawn and its black wrought-iron fence. In this house lived a pair of evil and sanctimonious twin boys who regularly vandalized my mother's tomato plants. I turned back up the hill of College Place, stopping at the Williams Inn gardens. Here I loitered for a while, sitting on the grass, waiting for Mr. Cartwright and Mr. Allen, two elderly Williams emeriti whose daily constitutional took them up that winding road. One was tall and courtly, with tortoise-shell spectacles, the other deformed, a near-dwarf with a built-up shoe and a face that sagged to the right. I intercepted them, and we had a little formal talk, Mr. Allen inquiring about my dog and my parents (never, bless him, a word about school!) and Mr. Cartwright managing with his tortured lips a remark about the weather. They stood over me, leaning in to hear my replies, and then continued on their halting way up the hill to the Williams Inn, where they took their meals.

What kind of people were my parents? Children can hardly be expected to place their parents on a sociohistorical map; this is a slow-arriving insight for most people, but especially for me, because between them my parents comprised so much cultural history and so much possibility. Each of them sat on a separate disordered burial mound of historical context. Trying to understand my parents, I've tried to understand the world.

Both were the children of children of immigrants; my mother grew up in Winnetka, Illinois, my father in Philadelphia. My mother's father represented the first generation of his family to achieve middle-class status; he was a banker. My father's father was a small-time math savant, able to do inventory in his head. He was the first of his generation to make money; he and my grandmother ran a lucrative brassiere and corset shop.

Both my parents were the elder of two children, and both were promising from birth, the repositories of their parents' most ambitious hopes. When they met at Swarthmore, they must have sensed the structural similarities of their circumstances even as they registered the intriguing differences. About their courtship I have a few jumbled impressions: My mother had recently been jilted by a man whose name I never learned; she spent a summer hospitalized with heavy uterine bleeding that she attributed directly to this emotional trauma. My father, sent back from his tenure as a Rhodes scholar at Oxford because of the war, proposed to my mother, then a teacher at Shady Hill school in Cambridge, Massachusetts, by lifting her over the River Charles and threatening to drop her.

My parents were married on Christmas Day in Winnetka; because my mother was Presbyterian and my father was Jewish, the ceremony was a civil one. The story about their wedding goes as follows: My father was in the army, stationed in Kansas, and he was due to arrive in Winnetka by train at noon. He was delayed. An office party was in progress at the courthouse, and my mother's father — ordinarily a respectable person — kept the offices open until my father's arrival by keeping the party going, dashing back and forth from the liquor store with bottle after bottle of spirits. My father's family was in attendance — even his elderly, diabetic, Yiddish-speaking grandmother — and I wonder what they made of all this.

Their married life began in Cambridge, and it was characterized by a lot of jolly and bibulous fraternization with a horde of rising young people, whose names I was to hear repeated all through my youth and some of whom, like my father, later figured in the Kennedy and Johnson administrations. My mother drew a series of cartoons celebrating incidents from their early married life. She called them the "piggy pictures." They are redolent of the period, delicately drawn and watercolored depictions of young people with the heads of pigs. The female pigs are slender and stylish in dresses with peplums and high-heeled mules; the males wear jackets to which my mother gave a textured, tweedy, academic appearance with tiny ink crosshatchings. I remember a Christmas piggy-picture sequence that my mother later framed, showing a semicircle of young pig carolers with hats and scarves and mittens, serenading a female pig on a balcony whose springy chestnut forelock identifies her as my mother. She is wearing a daring and flattering 1940s-style negligee set, and the carolers are singing "Some Holly for Molly" as musical notes float in clusters above their heads.

What fun, I suppose, though even now I can't help reacting to this with a child's scornful recoil. It makes me think of the mortification I suffered on the occasions—mercifully few—when my parents rolled up the rug in our living room and danced to Benny Goodman. Still, when I compare the optimistic bounce and élan of my parents and their friends in their youth to the yeasty solemnity of my own generation as we came of age, I must reluctantly admit that my parents were more attractive.

For years my parents' friends sent cards at Christmas; they covered the mantel, the coffee tables and end tables; when she ran out of surfaces, my mother pinned them to lengths of burlap and heaped them in ceramic bowls. So many friends, and the news conveyed in scrawled notes or mimeographed on attached sheets generally upbeat: children thriving, newly retired parents taking long-awaited cruises, Dorothy finding time for a pottery class now that our youngest is in half-day kindergarten. And as time passed and news began to darken, it was conveyed briskly and cheerfully: Patty back with us after a rocky semester at Bryn Mawr, but she'll soon be back at the books locally at the state university. Bob had a scare with his heart. After two hospitalizations and much back and forth with Blue Cross/Blue Shield, they tell us it was all a false alarm!

Much more and worse happened, of course, and not all of it was passed on in Christmas messages. My parents and their friends were as vulnerable to human misery as any other group, and they were visited by all the major forms of it—madness, illness, loss of love, and addiction, especially to alcohol. At the sober reception after my father's funeral and ecumenical memorial service, a group of my parents' friends huddled around my sister, there with her husband and small children. My sister tells me that these people approached her very earnestly and asked her questions about how she had managed to live so apparently well and happily. What renunciations, what settings-in-order had been necessary? (My sister's marriage ended a few years later.)

In recent years when my mother lived alone in a small condominium, the Christmas cards, though diminished in number, still kept coming. On my infrequent visits I passed the time by reading them. When my mother had withdrawn from conversation and sat in an armchair embroidering and smoking, and I had grown too restless to sit, I cruised the room, flipping these cards open and replacing them carefully. By then the messages had turned small and beseeching—Molly dear, do you remember? It seemed to me that age and debility had finally beaten the bounce out of these friends, brought them to some kind of honesty, some accounting. But for what? I was shocked at the vehemence of my satisfaction.

My parents' marriage was not happy, but it was loyal and successful, and more than any other marriage I can think of, it began with shared understandings. Implicit in my parents' marital pact was an agreement to cut themselves loose—the better to rise fast and far in a giddyingly new and open-ended intellectual meritocracy—from their respective moorings in cultural tradition and religious identification. Mine was a family in which a big bang of upward mobility had been detonated on both sides a few generations earlier. Its concentrated force shot my parents straight up into an empyrean of high achievement, but this explosion had lost energy in my generation. What remained of its force was dispersive rather than propulsive. The tendency was to come apart, to separate and fall away.

With their progressive views, their scorn for religion and filial piety, my parents were air plants, sustained by commonly held beliefs in reason, beauty, and their own superiority. My father more or less repudiated his own parents, especially his mother, a rather simple-minded woman who had been a beauty in her youth. By the time I knew her, she had turned querulous and bigoted in her widowhood. Stout and flatulent, insistent on being kissed, she was an object of dread. No prospect was more distasteful than a visit to her high-rise apartment in Philadelphia, where she knitted afghans and grumbled about "the colored" who had ruined her old neighborhood, and where I had to spread Louis Sherry sugarless jelly on my toast and sprinkle saccharin on my cereal. My grandfather, who died when I was a baby, was rarely mentioned, but I know that my father deplored his father's weakness for gambling on the horses and the stock market, and that he considered himself the responsible one in his family. My father's childhood was largely a blank to me; he almost never spoke of it except to tell stories about a dog that he and his brother owned, a prodigious German shepherd named Legs.

My maternal grandmother was a midwestern clubwoman with a triple row of chins. She was animated and easily flustered, with a tendency to make unfounded but emphatic generalizations, insisting, for example, that there were no piano players in Japan. My mother resented her mother and adored her father, a gentle man with a wry sense of humor and a habit of puncturing his wife's pronouncements with quietly voiced asides. He wore a tweed golfing cap and grew increasingly deaf in the years I knew him. My mother remained anxious for her parents' approval all her life. Until she died, and long after they had, she remained their nervous, witty, gifted, gallant little Molly.

My mother borrowed from her childhood—a rich, imaginative, and lonely one—the materials out of which she constructed mine. But even as a small child, I sensed that an essential context was missing, that all the pleasant objects and sensations of my childhood had been lifted out of a liquid suspension and handed to me, one by one, in a way that both pleased and bewildered me, and also made me feel a little ashamed of my greed. I've always been troubled by the obscure suspicion that if only I had been patient enough to let these gifts accumulate, to collect rather than consume them, I might eventually have been rewarded with a larger understanding of what they meant when reassembled. Even now I can't escape the feeling that I long ago ate my way through the legacy my mother intended for me.

Her attitude toward housework was healthily casual; hygiene was never the obsession for her that it is said to have been for 1950s housewives generally. But as—and how she hated this word—"homemaker," she was endlessly creative. When she bathed my brother and me, she floated birthday candles anchored in halved walnut shells in the bathtub. She turned off the lights, lit the candles, and stood smoking a cigarette in a shadowy corner of the bathroom as we sat in the midst of a small shining armada.

The productions of her kitchen were extraordinarily varied and inventive. For our birthdays we came to expect cakes baked in her lamb-shaped mold, covered with woolly coats of vanilla frosting and shaved coconut. Even for everyday meals she managed to get hold of ingredients nobody else seemed to find at our local A&P, exotic items like endives and shallots and avocados. Before a dinner party—hers were legendary—she spent the day making puff pastry, or feeding poached chicken livers into a meat grinder for pâté, or cutting radishes into roses with a freshly sharpened paring knife. I can see her clearly, in the kitchen or at her sewing table, stepping back momentarily from her task and breathing the half-frustrated, half-satisfied sigh of a perfectionist, one hand on her hip, the other absently smoothing the nape of her neck.

My mother created an extraordinary world for my brother and sister and me—an "enriched early environment" far beyond the requirements of any developmental psychologist—but she also left us with the disconcerting feeling that all the things she did were not done, entirely, for us. We were the occasion for their doing, as the play is the occasion for the labors of the set designer, but really they were done for their own sake; they were her art.

I was happiest when I could prevail on her to sit with me at the piano, playing songs from *The Fireside Book of Folk Songs* while I sang. One we often performed was "The Foggy Foggy Dew," that mystifying ballad of sorrowful craving, in which the fair young maid "wept and cried and tore her hair" in her longing for whatever it was that was hidden in the euphemism of the title. Another was "Funiculi, Funicula," which I enjoyed as much for the picture that accompanied it in the book, the snow-topped peak and cable cars suggesting the north of Italy and the pastiche evoking the south— the very full glass of very red wine, the grape arbor, and the fat brunette couple gazing into one another's dark eyes—as I did its words and melody.

My favorite was "The Minstrel Boy." This song brought to the surface all my finest feelings, all my ripest ardor, and I sang it with tears rolling down my cheeks. I especially loved the following verse, which I still know by heart:

The minstrel fell, but the foeman's chain
Could not bring that proud soul under.
The harp he loved never spoke again,
For he tore its chords asunder.

It was that last line that I found beautiful in a literary way. I responded to the satisfying pattern of long Os in "for" and "tore" and "chords," and most of all to the thrilling archaism "asunder," which suggested "thunder" and ended the verse with a rolling and portentous reverberation.

My mother sat at the bench and I stood beside her, warbling uninhibitedly while she pounded away at the old upright with the diligently anonymous air of a real accompanist. Behind us tall windows made of rippled old glass looked out on the chestnut tree in our side yard and beyond that, one of the white clapboard Williams Inn annexes, half hidden by tall trees and shrubbery, and invisibly beyond that, the town cemetery. These sessions at the piano were soul ventilations, and I remember my amazement at my mother's patience, and my grateful conviction that she understood exactly what I loved about these songs, that this was what she loved too, that she brought to mind as she played exactly the images that visited me as I sang. But I also remember my sense, something less than a suspicion but persistent nonetheless, that my mother was embarrassed by me and my quavering soprano and my tears.

Gradually, the belief I held so firmly in early childhood—that my mother and I shared some deep and exclusive understanding—began to erode, and I was left with the lifelong task of trying to figure her out. Even as a nine-year-old, I was inwardly engaged in the effort to define her aesthetic. Once, on our way back from North Adams, where we had spent an afternoon shopping for what we then called "dungarees" for me and my brother, we found ourselves driving into a spectacular pink and bronze sunset. "Nature," I ventured, hoping to please that puzzling aesthete, my mother, "is in bad taste."

For a while I had a Catholic friend whose mystifying observances piqued my curiosity about religion. My mother was reluctant to let me attend mass on a regular basis, but as a compromise, she let me go to Sunday school at the local Congregational Church. The class met in a sunny whitewashed room at the back of the church: One wall was covered with a child-executed mural on squares of butcher paper, showing the red, yellow, brown, and white children of the world, linked like paper dolls to encircle a globe. We sang Israeli and Greek folk songs, and our teacher glossed some of the tamer Bible stories. I was disappointed that we never got a chance to take on the parts of that book I found shocking and compelling, the Old Testament threats and tantrums. I was fascinated by this angry and irrational old God, torn between my covert attraction to Him and my indignation at His manifest unreasonableness.

I found the ecumenical ethos of the Congregational Church appealing and comforting; its universalist aesthetic was familiar to me from the homes of my parents' friends, the tacked-up children's drawings, the batik hangings and sisal rugs. But I also found it flat; I knew that in this bright, simple room I could find none of the winding rituals of initiation through which my Catholic friend was making her way, no chance for confession or absolution.

In my own house, my father's rational agnosticism was made palatable by my mother's aestheticized holiday Christianity. Just as she scooped out the thorny core of my artichoke, leaving the edible heart, so she separated belief and doctrine from the attractive rituals—the food and music and the familiar surfaces embellished and glittering—of her own childhood Presbyterianism. We spent two weeks before Christmas, my mother, sister, brother, and I, at the kitchen table, mixing food coloring into small bowls of vanilla icing—pale green, pink, a saturated shade I called chocolate blue. We used toothpicks to paint striped frosting trousers on the rudimentary legs of gingerbread men, buttoned up their blurred pastel waistcoats with silvery sugar balls. We collected pine cones and sprayed them, over newspaper, with silver and gold (the wonderful toxic reek of those spray cans, which were also preternaturally cold to the touch!); we saved the tops and bottoms of tin cans and used metal shears to cut them into stars and spirals for the Christmas tree. When we were very small, my mother allowed us to keep Advent calendars. We hung them in our bedroom window against the white winter light and opened a door each day, finding a translucent symbolic favor revealed—a pear, a sprig of holly, a mournful doll. The final door, a gold-encrusted flap three times the size of the others, opened to show the manger scene, but I can't picture it. Because of some tangle of neural strands, or the operations of an internal censor, I remember instead a miniature view of the Williams College skating rink.

We children learned nothing about Judaism, except a vague understanding that the corned beef sandwiches my father loved were Jewish. Also the cheek-pinching aunts we sometimes encountered in New York and Philadelphia, and the pickles my father despaired of finding anywhere locally and made himself from his grandmother's recipe, soaking Kirby cucumbers from my mother's garden in icy brine in a ceramic crock he kept in a corner of our unheated mud room—all these things were from the Jewish side of the universe, as were abstractions like justice and the gross national product. I understood as Jewish the sometimes coarse and jarring jokes and epigrams my father loved to repeat. A dog goes into a bar, they typically began. Maybe I should have said DiMaggio, they ended. I learned much later that my father was one of the first Jews to teach at Williams, where only a few years earlier a quota system had effectively kept them out.

My parents made strange bedfellows. In spite of the differences in their backgrounds, they faced the world in perfect alliance. Their politics were smoothly merged; they lived in a time when it was still possible to believe in human progress and they did, blithely and rather arrogantly, it seems to me now. My mother, as president of the local League of Women Voters, worked for the cause of fluoridation, which many local people considered a Communist plot. My father ran Adlai Stevenson's Berkshire office and also managed the campaigns of several local Democrats.

They believed in progress, not as an ideal but as an inevitability. This was the wave that had lifted and carried their immediate ancestors out of poverty and obscurity, and now my parents were riding it at its crest. Dim-witted superstition, prejudice, the forces of religion and reaction, extremism of any kind—these impediments were soon to be burned away by the light of reason.

Together, my parents made an unstoppable aesthetic-political flying wedge, she with her graces and accomplishments and her dinner parties, he with his intellect and the intimidating force of his presence. Without realizing it, my brother and sister and I lived in the broad, invisible end of the wedge, where it widened into the past, into separate and irreconcilable histories and traditions.

In me, the difficult child, the differences were enacted. My mother believed that knowing the beautiful meant knowing the right. To correct was clumsy and ill-advised. Surely, children brought up with good food and good literature and the example of beauty all around us would flourish and turn out well. My father—and here I perversely credit him with some parental feeling—saw that this was not happening, at least in my case.

He browbeat me unmercifully; he took out his tensions and frustrations on me, but I think he also acted from a genuine desire to teach. My mother protested to the degree her sense of fittingness allowed, and when her gentle intervention got her nowhere, she withdrew from both of us and, with a perfectionist's sense of failure, eventually from my brother and sister as well. I blundered into the widening space that separated my parents, to fall between them for years.

I remember my father best when he was in his early forties, around the time he took a job at the Ford Foundation and we left Williamstown for New York City. By then he was middle-aged; his hairline had receded, he was beginning to thicken around the middle, and pouches had formed under his eyes. It's always a small shock to look at early pictures and note again how handsome and noble-looking he had been only a few years earlier, tall and fair, with a high forehead, a Roman nose, and large contemplative eyes. In recent years I've wondered how much his Aryan looks had to do with his success, and I remember Dr. Farber's quick double take, when after more than three years as his patient, I happened to mention casually that my father was Jewish. I could sense that he was rapidly revising his view of me even as we sat there concluding the session, and that his opinion of my father, always mixed, had just swerved toward contempt. I think—

and here I'm reconstructing his view—that Dr. Farber was a little appalled at my father's failure to acknowledge his own Jewishness and to convey that recognition to his children.

My father had the mark of brilliance on him. He had the "coup d'oeil," an ability to see the whole panorama of an abstract landscape at once. He was quick and penetrating and intellectually gregarious but also harshly judgmental. Things happened so fast to my father that he never got around to completing his Ph.D., and he was so busy thinking—he would often sit at the dinner table in a kind of cataleptic trance, his eyes wide and blank, his jaw hanging—that he never produced a book.

Today, with these deficiencies, my father would be unable to get tenure at any university. And even then, he felt out of place in academic life. He had an itch for action, an impatience with circumlocution, a blunt and colorful sense of humor. He wrote so well, with such Senecan balance and clarity, that he paralyzed himself with his own high standards. Unable to produce much on the page, he lived in talk. My mother's dinner table was populated by my father's colleagues in the economics department and their kinsmen, the political scientists. They debated volubly and hilariously, but my father's voice was the dominant one. "Unsound," I would hear him pronounce. Or "abysmal, just abysmal."

He was a disastrous parent, worse than he deserved to be, deficient in self-knowledge and easily angered. When he turned to his children, he seemed unable to modulate the hearty cynicism with which he looked at the world. "Who is Jack Frost?" I asked at the breakfast table. "Friend of your mother's," he answered, and smirked into his coffee cup. He had some crudely Pavlovian notions about childrearing, very much at odds with my mother's enlightened ideas. I got the worst of them, because I was so clumsy and absent-minded. When I left soap on the edge of the sink instead of the soap dish, he stood over me and made me replace it properly, remove and replace it again fifty times. The same corrective was applied to all my other lapses: leaving the top off the toothpaste tube, forgetting to turn off lights, scratching the paint on the car when I parked my bike in the garage. His provisions for reward were equally crude; after a good day he would usher me into his study and solemnly place a quarter in my outstretched palm.

My father's word for me and my actions was "careless." My brother and sister were shrewd and strategic about my father; they knew how to anticipate his reactions and dodge his wrath. I continued all through my childhood to do the things that infuriated him, and he continued to use negative reinforcement in his efforts to train me. Stupidly, bullheadedly, my father and I kept at it until, at age nine or ten, I conceded and retreated. I got back at him later, when adolescence gave me a new head of steam. At seventeen, when I had come home late and drunk from a party and he met me scowling at the door, I ran up all five flights of our Washington townhouse shrieking with laughter, flicking off lights as I went, leaving him— he already had the heart condition that would kill him before he reached sixty—in the dark.

And some years later, when I had returned home from Riggs for a few weeks, my sister's Machiavellian boyfriend and I staged a Christmas Eve insurrection, a drama of confrontation at my mother's festive table. As the *buche de Noel* sat unserved in flickering candle-light on the sideboard, the boyfriend and I held him accountable for everything—for my mother's alcoholism, which by then was full-blown, for the Vietnam War that he abetted by supporting, for the general unhappiness of our family. My father left the table in tears. The boyfriend and I hugged each other in triumph, while my mother and brother and sister looked on in silent dismay.

By the time he was seven and I was eight, it was clear that my brother was turning out to be a good if unremarkable student. I was already failing, forgetting homework, losing books. I spent hours in the detention called study hall until it occurred to me that I could simply climb through an open window, hop a brook and clamber over a barbed-wire fence, tearing the crotch of my tights in the process, and be gone into the woods.

I seemed especially incapable of learning math. Sometimes, usually in the aftermath of a report card, my father would sit with me at the kitchen table after the dinner dishes had been cleared, writing out arithmetic problems with a sharpened pencil, big bold numbers, four problems to a page on a yellow legal pad. Then he would cross his arms against his chest and sit, waiting. I peered at the page, light-headed and hot-faced with anxiety and irritation. My mind skittered away from the numerals, unable even to engage the task of computation. My father sucked at his pipe. I knew he would lose his patience eventually, and I welcomed his exasperated hiss of breath because I knew it would be followed by the scraping of his chair as he rose from the table and retreated to his study.

Latency transformed me for the worse, and I became a pariah at school. I was fat and grubby, a shame-faced mumbler with a double row of teeth. I spent more and more time reading, or alone in the woods, talking to myself and acting out the parts of imagined dramas. I understood that there was no hope for the school situation, that my job was to endure and avoid and hope that I could grow myself out of my troubles.

If the child I was then were growing up now, she would be identified as suffering from low self-esteem. Her learning disability would be diagnosed and remediated. She would be counseled and given inspirational stickers to paste on her lunch box; she might well be medicated with antidepressants or stimulants. Concerned adults would hover over her, surrounding her on every side, leaving her no escape.

Perhaps all this was exactly what I needed, but even as an adult, I find the prospect makes me long for the open window and the woods. I was, I want to protest, a happy child! My happiness was in being of no account, being forgotten by preoccupied adults, having for practical purposes no gender. My happiness was freedom.

The truth is that sometimes we all were happy, a happy family. Periodically, some spell would lift from us and it would be as if we had always been happy. The great glass jugs that the milkman left on our cold kitchen porch would spontaneously pop their corks, and all of us at the breakfast table would laugh. Or my father would sing, basso profundo, his chin tripling on his shirtfront: "Rocked . . . in the cradle . . . of the . . . deep." Or my mother and I would take a short evening walk to the end of College Place to admire a crescent moon, and we would sing as we ambled:

> *Au claire de la lune,*
> *Mon ami Pierrot,*
> *Prete-moi ta plume,*
> *Pour ecrire un mot.*

Happiness challenges everything. It upsets causality, undermines explanation. Because we were sometimes happy, I can never make sense of my childhood.

*   *   *

Eventually I found companions, two brothers, David and Timmy, both faculty brats and school pariahs like me. Sometimes we were joined by a fourth friend, Roger, whose father worked at Cornish Wire in North Adams. Roger and his family lived in a small blue house in one of the first suburban-style developments in Williamstown. With my unconscious snobbery, I looked down on them. He was an introspective boy with a Dostoyevskian gloom about him, and he was already an autodidact, roaming the stacks of the college library. In the 1960s, Roger became a revolutionary and distributed Marxist pamphlets at Cornish Wire after his father had retired.

The four of us plunged into a shared imaginative world. We roamed the town, going far beyond the boundaries of my old mother-sanctioned paradise. We rezoned and renamed it: Indian Country was the area of brush and swamp that stretched between David and Timmy's house and the back road to Bennington. New Inverness was a sweep of rising meadow beyond it. We penetrated every college building and formulated elaborate initiation rituals that required sneaking out of our houses at night.

I found it easy to escape during my parents' parties, which were frequent. When the drone of anecdote and explosions of raucous laughter reached a certain pitch, I knew I could ease down the stairs and out the first-floor study window that my father kept open. I was often gone half the night and got caught only once, when I returned from a cave-exploring expedition to find the guests out on the hill next to the library searching for me with flashlights. It was past midnight, and some of them were giggling. I hid behind a hedge, but our German shepherd caught my scent, howled, and flushed me out.

During the football season, David, Timmy, Roger, and I fanned out under the bleachers and picked up dropped change. After alumni weekends we knew where to look for church-key openers and collected bags full. Once we found an obscene Polaroid snapshot, a headless naked woman sitting on a black-and-white tiled floor, perhaps in one of the Lehman Hall bathrooms, her legs spread to disclose pubic hair and vulva. We were unsure what to do with this prize; eventually we decided that I should keep it for the group. The theory was that a girl was less likely to get in serious trouble than a boy if such a thing were intercepted by a parent. I kept it under the blotter on my desk, taking it out to show to my brother, who held it gingerly by the edges and looked at it for a few moments without comment. Eventually it disappeared, and I knew my mother had found it.

Toward the end of our family's Williamstown days, David and Timmy's father ran for Congress against a Pittsfield Republican named Sylvio Conte. We were caught up in the exhilaration of this campaign, and for a summer it united my family. We hung streamers, distributed leaflets, baked sheet cakes, and decorated them with red, white, and blue icing. On Labor Day a rented donkey arrived from Albany in a special covered truck.

Andy, Timmy, David, Roger, and I did our part by singing campaign songs in front of the Williams Inn. My mother wrote out lyrics on a square of cardboard— "He's for me. He's for you. He's a candidate true blue!"—and we bellowed them over and over to the tune of "As the Caissons Go Rolling Along." A small group of puzzled patrons wandered out from the bar to listen.

Republicans were half-mythical villainous creatures in my childhood imagination; they were as humorless and wicked as the unsmiling Russian crew of the enemy submarine in *Run Silent, Run*

Deep. Even though, as I later realized, the Williams Inn itself was a nest of them, I was not aware of ever having met one. I was deeply shocked when Sylvio Conte won the election, appalled that this vulgar Republican with too many vowels in his name had so conclusively trounced the forces of enlightenment. This defeat was my first inkling that my parents' order was not a universal one, and that perhaps it would not always prevail.

My parents did not seem surprised, and neither did David and Timmy's father. In fact, they hardly seemed to take it seriously; as the disastrous returns came in, they made a party of it, huddling around the small screen of our newly acquired black-and-white television set with a pack of young faculty supporters, all of them drinking freely and laughing uproariously.

It was a few months later, in the fall of 1959, that we emptied the wedding-cake house and returned it to the college, packed our aquamarine Plymouth station wagon, and moved to New York, where my father had accepted a position with the Ford Foundation. As we drove by the pastures of Housatonic, cows looked up from their grazing to gaze at us. My mother turned to Andy and me—my sister was now away at boarding school—and said, "Children, this is the end of an era." I remember thinking my first consciously critical thought about my mother then; her teary eyes embarrassed me, and her pronouncement seemed stagy and portentous.

The only place I can recall clearly in our Riverside Drive duplex is the kitchen door, which opened onto the echoing back stairs leading down to the basement and the laundry facilities. I remember my mother backing into the kitchen through that door, yanking the portable grocery cart up the final step, shrugging off her coat with a sigh, and running her hand through her disordered curls, exclaiming at the force of the winter winds that howled up 116th Street from the Hudson, strong enough to lift a small woman right off her feet. That door was the port of commerce in our apartment, and to me it represented a shrunken token of the freedom to come and go that we had lost when we left Williamstown.

Like many people with active imaginations, my mother had little curiosity or sense of adventure. New York brought out all her fragility and fearfulness and also a certain resentment. The city utterly defeated her impulse to mold her surroundings; it was an overwhelmingly complex, hard-surfaced, already-made environment that imposed its own terms on its inhabitants.

It was in New York that I began to realize that my mother was shy. She had been a popular hostess in Williamstown and a central member of a loosely organized communitarian society of faculty wives. Here there were no friends or acquaintances whom she could expect to encounter in the course of her day, and left to her own passive devices, she made no effort to arrange the lunches and shopping expeditions that made up the social routine of Ford Foundation wives.

She had one New York friend, Nancy, a chic, self-dramatizing, generous woman whose ringing voice had a catch or a sob in it, a person unlike anyone I had ever met. She breezed in and out of our lives, trailing cologne and presents, and she made a project of helping my mother assemble a suitable city wardrobe. I remember sitting in a fitting room in Bergdorf Goodman or Saks, some store my mother would never have dreamed of entering on her own initiative, my schoolbooks piled on my lap, while my mother tried on a strapless cocktail dress—black silk moiré, with a tulip-shaped skirt. She stood in front of the three-way mirror, hands on her hips, turning one way and then the other, while Nancy, who was a good six inches taller, hovered over her, tugging at the bodice to adjust it. My mother studied her mirrored reflection, her eyes and twisting mouth confessing embarrassment, pleasure, consternation, and something like hopefulness. As I watched her under the fluorescent light, I was struck by how small and gracefully constructed she was, how unlike me, how bony in some places and abundant in others. I also noticed that her skin had recently taken on a touch of shrivel, like a peach that looks perfect in the bowl but wrinkles slightly when you hold it in your hand. She decided against that dress and rejected several others Nancy had chosen for her; all of them were lovely, she said, but really not for her. Nancy rolled her eyes and threw her hands toward the ceiling in a gesture of mingled exasperation and acceptance.

The move from Williamstown to New York, and subsequently to Washington, was a calamity for my mother, more so than for any of the rest of us. In Williamstown, she and my father had been a united force in the furthering of his career, but now that process had suddenly accelerated and the reins of control had been yanked from her hands. In New York, and even more so in Washington, her nerve and wit deserted her. She was like a singer with a lovely voice that enchants a drawing-room audience but fails to carry in an auditorium. Too self-deprecating to make any bid to establish herself as a New York or Washington hostess, she became and remained a passive and decorative wife.

She made two attempts at adaptation; the first was to develop a Lady Macbeth–style investment in my father's career. None of us realized the intensity of her vicarious ambition; the first evidence we saw of it came years later with her surprising collapse into angry tears when my father decided not to accept Lyndon Johnson's offer of a cabinet position. The second, a longer-term strategy, successful in its own limited terms and compatible with her growing bitterness and sense of failure, was to take on the ironic persona of the "invisible woman." She wrote several satirical pieces in this vein, describing White House parties where her head was inadvertently used as a tripod by press photographers. Later, in her widowhood, when she had moved from Washington to a condominium in Williamstown, she parlayed this view of herself into a regular column in the *Berkshire Eagle* and became something of a local celebrity.

At my new school, which was private and progressive, things went badly almost immediately. I was intrigued by the arty, intense, Semitic-looking students, excited by the freewheeling and sophisticated air of the place. But I also felt quite unequal to it; next to the socially precocious city children in my class, I was big and shy and underdeveloped, a small-town Sasquatch flushed from its lair and cornered.

When some pointed remark from a teacher or snide comment from a classmate penetrated the homesick dreaminess that was my only refuge, I flew into unprecedented rages. Called to the front of the class to identify Burma, I yanked too hard on the string of the world map above the blackboard, and it clanged to the floor in its heavy metal cylinder, hitting me glancingly on the side of my head as it fell. When a supercilious minnow of a girl in the front row laughed, I scooped up the whole apparatus from the floor and chased after her, out the door and down the corridor, roaring and weeping, brandishing the metal cylinder like a battering ram, until I was intercepted by two male teachers and half dragged, half carried, to the principal's office.

Both Andy and I came down with complaints that my mother judged to be psychosomatic. Something in Andy's inner ear went awry, causing him to stagger when he walked. I developed a spastic colon and a rapid heartbeat. I can remember the stomach pains only faintly, but I do recall the Upper West Side offices of Herman Tannenbaum, M.D., where I was asked to remove my shirt, to breathe and hold the breath, and then to breathe again, while Dr. Tannenbaum cupped my shoulder in his overly warm palm and pressed a cold metal wafer into various regions of my back. Andy and I both got over our ailments, but I was the one to find myself in the office of Dr. V.

3

MY FIRST THERAPIST

*D*r. V was my first therapist, a classically trained Viennese psychoanalyst with a Park Avenue address. Two days a week, after school, I climbed onto a city bus at 110th Street and went rattling south along Fifth Avenue past the newly erected Guggenheim on my left and Central Park on my right.

The bus was half empty at that hour; a gritty, city-scented wind swept through its open windows. We passed doormen with epaulets of gold braid standing guard in squares of awning shade, and women of indeterminate age in turbans and bedroom slippers, minks thrown over their dressing gowns, walking small dogs in plaid jackets.

This was the quiet time of the afternoon, just before four. What I could see of the park looked deserted; a chestnut vendor had temporarily abandoned his cart and his charred oven mitts and sat resting on a bench. The winter twilight would arrive while I lay on Dr. V's couch; soon the turbaned ladies would ascend to their apartments, to bathe and perfume themselves in preparation for unimaginable evenings.

I kept an eye on two of my schoolfellows who rode that bus to the offices of their own therapists. The three of us arranged ourselves as far away from one another as the seating on the bus allowed. By the time I had reached my stop, the other two had separately disembarked, swinging down to the street and tossing their green baize book bags over their shoulders with enviable urban panache.

Dr. V's waiting room was small and windowless and unremarkable except for its salient feature, a large tank of tropical fish, lit cloudily from within. I'm sure I was not the only patient who felt compelled to kneel in front of that aquarium, drawn by the lulling glide and flicker of the fish on their regally pointless circular travels.

I heard the other door of Dr. V's office creak open and creak shut as she ushered the patient who preceded me into the hall. I knew then to collect myself and my book bag, to get up from the floor and seat myself in one of two armchairs stiffly upholstered in royal blue brocade, and prepare myself for the moment when she appeared to usher me into her treatment room.

I was to remain Dr. V's patient for only a year. When my father was summoned by the newly inaugurated President Kennedy to join his Council of Economic Advisers and we moved to Washington, she was replaced by Dr. H, also a woman, also a classically trained psychoanalyst. Unlike Dr. V, she was an American midwesterner and smoked. Like Dr. V, she put me on the couch and maintained a silence through the hour.

But she knitted me a sweater. The cables fell out of her needles fully articulated, like great ropes heaved length by length over the side of a ship. I appreciated the symbolism; the developing sweater was meant to suggest that something was being made here, that in spite of my nearly complete silence, progress of some kind was happening. That therapy also ended within a year, and without explanation.

I failed in these early therapies, or attempts at analysis, as I suppose they should properly be called. How could I have succeeded? And what could Drs. V and H have been expecting? Thrown into deep waters without instruction, I floated mute. My silence was both anxious and voluptuous. I felt a gentle pressure to speak, but I also felt pillowed by the assurance that silence was all right—good, in fact. It established my bona fides as a sensitive person, because only a sensitive person would remain silent when given the opportunity to speak. The more silence, the more certainty that the surface tension of the silence would break; the more prolonged the silence, the more import it would be seen, once broken, to have had. The first would be last and the last would be first: I had internalized this, the fundamental psychoanalytic dialectic, before I turned thirteen. On the couch I felt like a passenger on a gently rocking bed, traveling somewhere by train, passive and inert, but hurtled forward by the process of travel.

The waiting rooms of Drs. V and H had the feeling, for me, of sanctified space. I understood Dr. V's aquarium as a metaphor for the mind: those glittering bits of protein flashing through it—how I wished I could pinch the tails of their analogs in my brain, draw them out wriggling, and present them to her. And the framed reproduction of Rouault's little king that dominated Dr. H's waiting room seemed to me the focal point of a shrine.

I brought a free-floating ardor to my first encounters with therapy, a kind of religious hunger that had gone unfed by my parents' agnosticism, their skepticism, their pragmatic liberalism. As I lay on the couch, my thoughts were runnels of dreamy speculation just below the translucent skin of consciousness, monitored but not entirely registered. I never actually expressed these thoughts, not because I was secretive but because I had misunderstood the rules of free association. Somehow I had picked up the idea that only unconscious thoughts were to be spoken—an obvious contradiction, but I blurred this impossibility into a kind of Zen koan. Once I had solved it, I felt sure that enlightenment would follow.

A few years after Dr. H came Dr. G, the first male. He was the most genuinely detached of all my therapists. I had just turned sixteen a few weeks before I first walked into his office, and when I remember him, I bring to mind a cartoonist's doodle-drawing of a shrink—one quick unbroken line describing a domed, balding head, continuing with a substantial hooked nose and receding chin, and petering out after tracing the swell of a modest professional's paunch. He had a wry decency that was mostly, but not entirely, lost on me at the time.

My therapy with Dr. G was the first in which I sat up and faced the therapist, the first in which I talked freely, and also the first in which I withheld or distorted the truth. I never mentioned how mortified I was, for example, to notice that the patient who exited his waiting room as I entered was a fat obnoxious girl from my school with alopecia and a steady rapid blink.

With Dr. G, I learned to "talk therapy." This was not a matter of using jargon—I'm proud to say I've never done that—but of recognizing which gambits and attitudes cause the therapist to signal his receptiveness. Even the most poker-faced practitioner will often reward an attentive patient with some small sign, a subtle alteration in the set of facial muscles, a dilation of the pupils. With Dr. G, I reached the "clever Hans" stage of my development as a patient.

And like the novice painter who has learned to use the entire canvas, I finally learned how to fill the hour; now I saw that any-

thing I said could be depended on to color the silences that followed, giving them a plausible opacity behind which I could hide
until I found another thing to say. I discovered that dreams were
listened to attentively. I often spoke about loneliness, or feeling as
if I were enclosed in a glass box. These themes seemed to engage
Dr. G, and they gave me a pleasant feeling too. I enjoyed the waif-
like image I conjured up of myself, and the resultant gentle tide of
self-pity that washed over me, raising the hair on my arms and
leaving my eyes prickling with tears.

Throughout my years as Dr. G's patient, I felt a guilty and
unshakable conviction that I was completely sane and that I had
health to squander. Of course, my notion that patients were
expected to be crazy was naive, but I had swallowed whole the familiar ideology that connects madness to beauty of spirit. My knowledge of my strength and sanity was a secret I did my best to keep
from Dr. G. I wanted him to see me as vulnerable and sensitive
rather than robust. I loved the notion of myself as saucer-eyed and
frail, and I was ashamed of the blunt and caustic person I knew I
was. I hoped that if I applied myself, I might evolve toward becoming the fragile and lovable being I so wished to be. I was looking for
transformation, not cure. I wasn't interested in being happier but in
growing more poignantly, becomingly, meaningfully unhappy.

Why so many therapies, and why so early? My mother would
have explained that my chronic underachievement in school was
the reason, and later she would have added my bad and wild behavior (mild by today's standards). And what was wrong with me? A family-systems therapist would have identified me as the family scapegoat, the child designated to "act out" the conflicts between my
tense, driven father and my incipiently alcoholic mother, the vent
through which the collective rage escaped; a Winnicottean would

point to the consequences of early maternal inadequacy (my mother was bedridden with phlebitis for most of my first year); a practitioner with a neurological bent could find evidence of a learning disability.

All these hypotheses have explanatory power. I tend to favor the last one, at least on days when I feel inclined to believe that there *is* such a thing as a learning disability. But they were all equally irrelevant to the subjective reality of the adolescent I was. About her, I can only say that if she was angry, she was also extremely passive and mired in helplessness, and that therapy became a means by which she became even more so.

I believe that my early therapies did me harm. They swallowed up years when I might have been learning, gathering competence and undergoing the toughening by degrees that engagement in the world makes possible. But worse than this was the effect of my therapies on my moral development: Seedlings of virtues withered. An impulse that might have flowered, for example, into tact, fell on the stony ground of the therapist's neutrality and became manipulativeness, a tough perennial better suited to these desert conditions.

By the time Dr. G and my parents sent me to Austen Riggs, I had acquired the habit of the analysand, the ruthless stripping away of defenses. But in my case not much self had yet developed, and surely none of it was expendable. I was tearing away not a hardened carapace but the developing layers of my epidermis. By reducing myself to a larval, infantile state, I was doing what I felt I was expected to do, and what would please the therapist.

My early therapists were doctrinaire in a way that seems almost quaintly anachronistic. No eleven-year-old child is made to lie on an analytic couch today, or even to sit up in a chair, facing a silent, nondirective therapist across an expanse of oriental rug. My concern is not with these therapists—I realize now that even forty years ago, they and their kind were beginning to be seen as living fossils. Instead, my questions are addressed to the broader body of thought and practice they rigidly and inappropriately applied to my case. And my doubts about therapy extend further still—beyond psychotherapeutic theory and practice to the ubiquitous culture of therapy that surrounds us all, and from which there is apparently no escape.

But let me return to Dr. V. She was a tall, plump, middle-aged woman with oddly mismatched eyes. One was small and weepy; the other was unnaturally large, unblinking and glaucous, like an eye behind a jeweler's loupe. I developed a theory that the small eye was diseased and the big one had become hypertrophied in taking over its function. Now it seems more likely that the big eye was sightless, and the small one soon to become so.

Dabbing at her discharging eye with a handkerchief, she ushered me into her office. With a series of smooth movements, so ritualized that a choreographer might have blocked them out, she walked me to the couch and withdrew to her own chair, where she sat silently, just out of my view, until the end of the session, which she signaled by clearing her throat and rising to her feet.

The couch was actually an armless and backless chaise longue, upholstered in a stiff tweed fabric. I lay down and arranged myself as modestly as I could, making sure my knees were covered by my pleated plaid skirt. I rested my head on a square of crackling plastic, a hygienic reminder of the heads of Dr. V's other patients. I crossed my ankles, folded my hands on my chest, and rolled my eyes up to the ceiling; in the early months I spent the first few minutes of every session fighting an almost overpowering urge to giggle.

It seemed that one of the rules of this game was that none

were given. I knew that the patient was expected to speak, and that the analyst remained mostly silent. I assumed the patient came to the office spring-loaded, ready to release an accordionated narrative of passion or anger. But I could find nothing pressurized inside myself, nothing dynamic.

Sometimes I entertained fantasies in which I—or a kind of stand-in for me—rose from the couch and paced the room talking and gesturing volubly, pausing to gaze moodily out the window, as I had seen characters do in movies. I imagined that movement would free my paralyzed tongue, but when I dwelt on the fantasy I understood that my self-dramatizing doppelgänger had nothing real to say, only stock phrases—"I've had it up to here!" or "I can't take it anymore!"—uttered emphatically but free of any of the content of my life.

The only sound in the office was the steady scratching of Dr. V's fountain pen as she wrote. Wrote what? A poem? A story? A grocery list? A letter to another psychoanalyst? Sometimes it seemed plausible to me that she had access to my unspoken thoughts, and it was those that she was transcribing through the hour. But why? To pass the information along to my parents? It seemed unlikely that they would place high value on it; it was I, after all, who was continually dogging my mother around the kitchen, talking her ear off. And how—here was my first articulation of a question that has plagued me ever since—could Dr. V manage to find words for my thoughts, the deepest and least voluntary of which came to me as pictures accompanied by impressions impossible to characterize but bearing some resemblance to odors or musical chords?

My attitude toward Dr. V, and psychoanalysis in general, was a primitive amalgam of fascination and fearful suspicion, something like the feelings of a Trobriand islander who holds a squawking transistor radio to his ear. I had had one previous exposure to the world of psychology; four years earlier, while we still lived in Williamstown, my mother had taken me to be tested by a psychologist, a man with a yellow tie, in the nearby mill town of North Adams. He invited me to play checkers, an obvious loosening-up ploy, perhaps with some obscure diagnostic purpose. Then he asked me to draw pictures of the members of my family and seemed nonplussed when I asked if that included my dog. I knew why I was there—consistently failing grades in every subject but English. I also knew quite well that no grown man in a tie, yellow or otherwise, would spend a weekday hour playing checkers with an eight-year-old without some ulterior motive, nor would he keep an office in the basement of North Adams State Teachers College simply to amuse himself by watching children draw pictures. I knew I was being evaluated, but whether it was my intelligence or my sanity—or both—that was in question, I couldn't tell. Actually I feared something else was being judged, something about myself I couldn't comprehend, and I also feared that in the course of the investigation, I would be left open to some shameful exposure. In order to discover whatever it was about me that he wished to know, he would need to unfurl me and read me like a scroll.

I judged the silence in Dr. V's office to mean that we had bypassed, or at least deferred, the terrors of diagnosis. I was grateful for that. After a few months I began, hesitantly, to enjoy my sessions on the couch, to take them as a holiday from the exclusively verbal means by which I engaged the world.

Certainly there were many things I would have liked to talk about, with someone other than Dr. V. I would have enjoyed describing the two sophisticated girls at school, eighth graders with bohemian airs who had surprised me by befriending me, who seemed to find intriguing some of the very traits that had made me a pariah in my old school. Perhaps I might even have gotten some relief by exorcising the business about my teacher, the bouncy, intrusively concerned young man we called Hal—he was the first person I ever saw twirl a chair around and straddle its seat backward—who kept me for counseling sessions after class. He mortified me once, in the course of helping me on with my jacket, by discovering two wads of candy-bar wrappers I had stuffed into its pockets. "What's this?" he cried. "Oh, what's this?" and we had to sit down again while he made a reproachful inventory, uncrumpling each wrapper, flattening it with the heel of his palm, and holding it up to me. Milky Way: Had I found eating this helpful? Sky Bar: Had it improved my life? Three Musketeers: Was I any happier for it?

But none of this was located at the right depth for expression in Dr. V's office. Her silence and her affliction gave her the air of a prophetess, and I felt that my hurts and joys were too specific, too real, too much rooted in the embarrassing actualities of my life to be expressed to her. My understanding of psychoanalysis was cultic, shot through with magic, and it seemed safest to answer Dr. V's mute eloquence with an imitative silence.

I knew I was incurring a debt, and that when I finally did speak, what emerged would have to be something very big and dark and grandly dramatic. Nothing less could drain the deepening pool of silence.

My family spent our first non-Williamstown Christmas in Puerto Rico. We had never done anything like this before, and I took it as a measure of my mother's despair about New York that she was willing even to contemplate such a venture.

We took a late-night budget flight to San Juan from what was then Idlewild Airport. I remember standing for at least half an hour with my parents and brother and sister in one of many long swaying lines of bulky travelers, burdened with packages and luggage. Suddenly we felt a ripple of passage in the line and saw that a man in a belted camel's-hair coat was being ushered rapidly to the front by a stewardess. My father broke ranks to follow him, and I felt my mother stiffen. My father tapped the man on his shoulder and when he turned, punched him squarely on the chin, hard enough to make him keel over into the arms of the crowd, where he lay propped like a felled tree in a dense forest, his legs splayed stiffly. Some in the crowd groaned with shock and disapproval, but more cheered. My father returned to us, still seething with hot principled indignation. This man, he explained, had bribed the stewardess to bring him to the front of the line.

That was not the last man I saw my father hit. He had a pugilistic streak, most unexpected in a Keynesian economic theorist; some years later I saw him take a swing at a car salesman. In that case, the blow went wide, grazing the man's cheekbone as he dodged, and causing my father to lose his balance and stagger clumsily.

The plane was hot, packed, and smoky. I was seated behind my parents, and in the middle of the night I woke to see my mother staring at me blankly over the back of her seat; she was kneeling, her chin propped on her folded arms. Something about the sight of her in such an uncharacteristic and childlike pose frightened and disoriented me, and to my great shame I found that tears were rolling down my face. My mother whispered that she was stiff from sitting and that changing her position made her more comfortable, but my tears continued.

The next morning I stood up from the toilet in our rented beach cabin and looked down into a bowl of red water. I can't say that I was unprepared for this event; my mother had given me the full explanation at least a year earlier; she had even drawn—with pink, purple, and maroon colored pencils—a diagram of the ovaries and fallopian tubes and uterus. But apparently I had failed to absorb the information, or stored it in some inaccessible part of my brain, because the shock of seeing this unprecedented color made me wail for my mother. Through the plywood partition that separated the bathroom from the rest of the cabin, I heard my father, who was still in bed, laugh hoarsely. "There goes another one," he said.

We stayed for a few days in this primitive seaside resort, sleeping under mosquito netting. We ate in a small restaurant owned by the proprietor; our breakfasts consisted of slabs of fresh pineapple, served with a flourish on heavy white china by a grubbily uniformed waiter, and small cups of thick black coffee. My mother taught me to use a pad and a sanitary belt, and I was bitterly disappointed that I was unable to swim. I felt disoriented and woozy, but I was also enchanted by the reach of lawn that swept down from our cabin to the seawall and the beach, by the palms and the cascades of bougainvillea and the flowery morning breezes. I associated the seductive loosening of feeling that people succumb to in the tropics with my new menstruating condition; about that I felt an almost uncontainably volatile combination of secretive pride and angry embarrassment.

We drove across the island to another hotel where my parents had made reservations for Christmas Eve. I found the interior of the island nightmarish, hot and hilly and clotted with garish vegetation, senselessly profuse, one thing growing out of another into a canopy so dense that even the memory of the underlying soil was lost. I had never missed Williamstown more intensely. I pictured it as it looked just after the autumn leaves had fallen and blown

away, not the muffled snowy Christmas but the revealed and
denuded landscape of Thanksgiving, the blue, gray, gold, and vio-
let palette of late November.

Williamstown, I was thinking, was a *decent* place, where a thing
was itself and not another thing. It was a place where thoughts could
be separate and fully formed, where each had room to rise and float
away from its fellow thoughts, which here seemed to merge and
engulf one another. I imagined that my family had gone into exile,
and that our fate was to be trapped together forever, in our apartment in alien New York City or in a tiny rental car making its way
across this unassimilable island.

I watched my mother for clues to her state of mind, but the back
of her head was quite composed and uncommunicative as the car
rose and dipped through the inland jungle. We arrived at our desti-
nation on Christmas Eve, a squalid little town where pigs were
herded through the streets. The hotel was modern and so new that
two sides of it sat unlandscaped in a flat field of dried mud.

A brace of piglets was being roasted on a spit by the swimming
pool in preparation for the evening festivities. At dusk the shrubbery around the pool began to twinkle with lights. My parents had
drinks by the pool, and we listened to some elderly midwesterners
sing Christmas carols, accompanied by a ukelele. A clowning
tourist jumped into the water fully dressed in chinos and madras
jacket. My father laughed. My brother and I, little puritans that
we were, both glared indignantly.

Later that Christmas Eve — or was it the next night? — we went
on a boat ride in the harbor. The water was full of tiny phospho-
rescent creatures; a hand or foot dipped into it came out glowing
and glittering. My mother found this fascinating; again and again,
as my father sat at the rudder, she lowered her hand into the

water, held it up loosely in front of her eyes, and gazed at it. I was to observe this sequence of actions and this expression many times in the years to follow. She would often do something similar at the dinner table in Washington, holding up her graceful, aging hand so that it was framed by the nimbus of the candle flame, turning it this way and that and marveling as if it had been transformed into the head of a swan. I learned to note the marks of intoxication in the slowness of her movements, the puzzled tilt of her chin, her wistful, solipsistic half-smile.

Some months after our return from Puerto Rico, in the early spring, I began to dare to like New York. I liked it a little guiltily, because it seemed a betrayal to like this place that my mother found so oppressive. In fact, I liked about it exactly what my mother hated—its impersonality, multiplicity, and strangeness. In Williamstown I had been able to wander far afield, but in New York I realized that even the daily ride to school along 110th Street offered me a new and radical freedom. Once I had learned to sink into the anonymity that the city offered to all its inhabitants, I could become entirely what for years I had been tending toward being—an observing eye. I took to this condition with a natural and delighted relief.

I might, for example, look from my seat on the bus to see a little dark woman with a rosy caste mark on her forehead, huddling miserably at the bus stop in a man's tweed coat many sizes too big for her. I had only the sketchiest frame of reference in which to place this woman—I knew she was Indian, and that was all—but my imagination would squeeze a kind of squid's ink of longing into the emptiness of my speculations about her; I would feel a painful, exhilarated desire for everything I could not yet know, all the smells and colors the world had not yet disclosed to me.

By the spring term, the two bohemian girls had become my friends. Now I had converted my generalized longings into the currency of female friendship by developing my first serious crush on a boy, a short strutting ninth grader with an Italian last name and theatrical ambitions. He was the subject of many long phone conversations; even the faintest of his smiles were logged and analyzed.

These friends took everything, including me, with great seriousness, and they introduced me to the idea of a life both private and intensely social, an abstract web of complex human circumstance that spread itself across the city. This was existence sorted by meaning, not crudely by locale: I learned about other students who had multiple admirers or petit mal epilepsy or genius IQs, or whose parents were divorcing. One of my new friends had a precocious gift for tact. When I asked her to tell me honestly whether she thought it was possible that the Italian boy might like me back, she replied, "Emily, it would take somebody very special to appreciate you."

I began to get to know the world of my Jewish relatives in New York—my father's widowed aunt Helen and her son, my cousin Dick, who was then in his late twenties, still living uneasily at home. Dick was a jazz aficionado and an incipient paranoid schizophrenic. He was the first hip person I ever knew, a romantic figure in his tight, tapered pants and narrow-toed Italian shoes, a small, elegantly slender man with a halo of kinky hair and large, heavy-lidded eyes.

My mother compared him to a Semitic prince, and I found him fascinating. He spoke in an intimate mumble; his smile was quick, wry, and confiding, and he stood very close to people when he talked. Once he took me to the Five Spot in the Village to listen to jazz. He bought me a whiskey sour, my first drink, which I finished with some effort and then threw up just as I was getting off the subway. On another occasion, when his mother was out of the apartment, he put a Sarah Vaughan record on the phonograph, pulled me to my feet, and danced with me, his arms draped languidly around my neck.

Dick was an N.Y.U. dropout without a job, a night person. His first psychotic break had occurred a few years earlier; just after his father's funeral he became convinced that his mother had given the key to her apartment to a cabal of his enemies. He tore the phone out of the wall and threatened her with a knife. Years later, when I lived in New York as an adult, he showed up periodically at my Inwood apartment. By then he was making sense only intermittently. He was grizzled and dirty, and he paced and smoked and coughed continually. When he was out of the hospital, he spent his days wandering Manhattan, reading coded messages on license plates and sleeping in parks. Antipsychotic drugs had left him with tardive dyskinesia, which made him lick his lips and swallow compulsively. He died a few years ago; I'm not sure how. I still own a little book of Oscar Wilde epigrams that he gave me on my thirteenth birthday.

I spent many evenings sitting at the dining room table in my great aunt's four-room apartment near Columbus Circle, while she fed me like a Strasbourg goose, scuttling back and forth from her tiny kitchen in her stocking feet, fetching me one whim after another—Coca-Cola with lots of ice, a dish of rice pudding, another slice of that brisket we had eaten for dinner an hour earlier. Conversation with my aunt was a little difficult; I took offense at her well-meaning inquiries about my "little friends," and her smiling, nodding, emphatic incomprehension when I tried to reply. I found it jarring when she referred to my mother as "Mother"—"does

I propped myself on my elbows and twisted my head to look at Dr. V and at the empty armchair by the window where I assumed my father had sat during his visit.

"I asked him to come," she went on. " Sometimes I like to have a chat with the parents." She paused. I stayed propped.

"Your father," said Dr. V, her voice rising into a lilt. "Do you know, I liked him?"

I sat up and turned toward her. Her face had spread into a radiant, moist smile, and I realized that she was telling me she found my father attractive. As I looked at Dr. V, I realized that this was the first time I had maintained a full frontal view of her for longer than a few seconds at a time.

What I saw now was a comfortable, maternal woman, perhaps a little sentimental in a European kind of way, cozily ensconced in her corner armchair, surrounded by small tokens of comfort my peripheral vision had never quite picked up—a silver-framed triptych of tiny oval photographs on her chairside table, a box of tissues, a small mirrored carousel holding an assortment of prescription pills, a beaded glasses case.

This was not the empress of silence! This was somebody very grounded and rather limited, and suddenly I realized that the silence in her office had never been magical, but rather one in which I lay on her couch in my rumpled school clothes, an inch or two of pudgy midriff exposed by the gap between my blouse and skirt waistband, paralyzed by self-consciousness, in full view of this half-blind woman who sat invisibly in her chair, feeling sorry for me.

"He was very much concerned about something. Would you like to know what it was?"

No, no, I wouldn't. It was all I could do not to stuff my fingers in my ears and drown out her voice with a howl of rage and panic.

"He was concerned about your weight. He would like to know why you have this problem of overeating. Do you know what I said to him? I pointed to his cigarette . . . ." Dr. V reproduced her gesture and then my father's reaction, his startled examination of his cigarette and his shrug.

"Why does he smoke? I asked him this." She broke off and mused for a moment, as if this were a natural resting place in her anecdote. Her hands were folded in her lap; her feet, in boat-shaped pumps, were propped on her embroidered footstool.

She continued. "Your father thought for a few moments. Clearly, he gave it some thought. And then . . ." Bending from the waist, Dr. V pantomimed the emphatic stubbing out of a ciga-rette, "he put . . . it . . . out."

4

A THERAPEUTIC EDUCATION

I n the fall of 1961, my family moved to Washington, D.C. We all attended my father's swearing-in ceremony and a reception at the White House. We stood in a receiving line to meet President Kennedy, the first lady, and the vice president, who took my hands in his large ones and leaned down to murmur, "How do you do, my little cottontailed bunny rabbit?" I wore a black-and-white checked shirtwaist with oversized pink rosette buttons that my mother had ordered from the "chubbette" section of the Sears catalogue. We ate petits fours, and my brother was forced to dance with me as the Marine Band played "The Syncopated Clock."

For a year my family sublet a furnished split-level at the end of a cul-de-sac in Bethesda, Maryland. The decor was Danish modern; the walls were painted unfamiliar colors like teal blue and olive green, the floors covered with wall-to-wall shag carpet. The place had an impersonal, fitted-out feeling, as if the rooms had all been furnished with one day's shopping. I was anxious for my mother the moment I saw it; surely this was worse than the Riverside Drive apartment, particularly the kitchen, with its teak mug rack and its breakfast nook and its gimmicky appliances. Her reaction was grim and businesslike; she inspected these new quarters like a squadron commander billeted to a wretched farmhouse, and lost no time setting up our household inside it.

I overheard my father speculating that our neighbor on the right was a "spook"—worked for the CIA—and when I remember that man's pallor and his haunted eyes as he went about his yard chores, my father's remark makes sense. Across the street was a family of Cuban émigrés with three teenaged daughters who trawled the neighborhood for makeover candidates; every weekend they appeared at our door, begging my mother for permission to curl my eyelashes and set my hair on rollers.

All over the development new houses were going up; the whine of saws and the thud of hammers were constant, and the smell of fresh lumber and paint was everywhere. But the circle of houses at the end of this cul-de-sac was still surrounded by woods, and once again I reverted to my old pattern of wandering in them. The Maryland woods were dense, prickly, and unwelcoming, full of tangled vines and poisonous plants, a different proposition from the benign New England woods I knew.

I followed a bulldozer track one hot Saturday afternoon, and to my surprise I stumbled upon a wide, slow-flowing river. I took off my clothes and waded in from the muddy bank, floated on my back, gazing up at a patch of milky sky through a cone of converging tree trunks. I knew this was a risky and slightly perverse thing I was doing, very much in keeping with the feeling of these rank southern woods, and also with the bold and careless depredations of the redneck men who drove the earth-moving behemoths that every day encroached upon them further, and as I flattened my chin on my chest, the better to admire the way my small breasts rose out of the water, I gave myself a reptilian sexual thrill. I heard a crackling noise from the direction of the bulldozer track, scrambled up onto the bank, desperately stuffed myself into my clothes, and ran. The next morning I was covered with a violent rash, an allergic reaction to poison ivy or sumac or oak—the doctor couldn't say which.

My mother enrolled me in the local public junior high, where I felt more conspicuously freakish than ever before. This was an accurate judgment; in my corduroy jumper and orthopedic oxfords, I was now objectively and unmistakably a misfit. I was surrounded by girls who carried ratting combs and cans of hair spray in their purses. They wore pastel flats and panty hose and skirts hemmed three inches above the knee, and every one of them seemed to have enlisted a boy to steer and pivot her through the halls, one hand flattened on the small of her back.

How did these girls manage their immaculate self-presentation?—by spending ten minutes before and after every class in the ladies' room. They packed the space in front of the mirror, the high-status girls in the first rank, the rest standing on tiptoe and craning their necks, applying mascara, covering blemishes with dots of foundation, tweaking, rubbing, and smoothing their faces into an acceptable condition. There was real discipline in this vigilant self-maintenance. And there was camaraderie in the girls' collective and competitive self-deprecation; they groaned about puffiness, shine, enlarged pores. One bold and popular girl even drew attention to her facial hair problem. No, the others cried. We can't see a thing! Look closely, she said, pointing to her upper lip. This is where I have to tweeze, every morning, yes I do, and the girls gathered around her with respectful acknowledging murmurs. I saw that the currency here was not natural beauty or skill at maquillage, but a knowledge of oneself as one appeared from the outside, and a capacity for unillusioned self-assessment. For this, one got the group's respect; for neutralizing envy by confessing one's defects, one got its love.

I saw immediately that this new school was an untenable situation for me, and my solution was the usual one. Whenever possible, I simply walked away from the bus stop into the woods, or, alternatively, I would sometimes continue down the road a few miles to Glen Echo Amusement Park—the scene of a recent and soon-to-become notorious race riot—where I would spend the day reading and people-watching at a wooden table outside one of the food concessions. This escape was feasible only three days a week, because on Tuesday and Thursday afternoons my mother picked me up at school and drove me to the office of my new therapist, Dr. H, the knitter.

This is how I remember the mother of my adolescence, the woman behind the wheel in sunglasses and a scarf, her face unreadable in profile, her pale arms covered with an odd growth of long downy hair—how I noticed every change in her aging, and how critical I was! In New York my mother had been thrown off balance and made vulnerable; in suburban Maryland she retreated into inaccessibility.

This was the mother of the long silences, driving from errand to errand. All through the years in Washington, I sat with her as she waited to make left turns, impatiently shaking one cigarette after another from the pack she kept on the dashboard—my parents smoked Kents now, no longer the filterless Lucky Strikes of the

Williamstown years—lighting and exhaling with a harsh sigh. In my mind I ran through a series of conversational openers, all the while queasily conscious that my anxious desire to know what was going on in my mother's mind was exactly a reversal of the normal. It was adolescents who were supposed to be inscrutable—wasn't it?—and their parents who were clumsy and intrusive.

Mrs. Striker, my home economics teacher, was often a good conversational gambit. My mother enjoyed my anecdotes about this woman, with her two bright spots of rouge and her resolute cheeriness, who taught us to make a sandwich without ever touching the bread or the filling, and instructed us in proper conversational etiquette at the table—no discussion of politics or religion or any controversial topic that might interfere with digestion. I had heard my mother repeating Striker stories to my father during the cocktail hour. Sometimes a new one—I was not above inventing them—would raise a smile, other times not.

My mother dropped me off in front of Dr. H's Georgetown brownstone. I made my way around the side of the house along a twisting brick pathway through an overgrown rose garden to the three stone steps that led down to her basement office. This approach always made me think of a fairy tale, an impression maintained when Dr. H opened the door to her tiny waiting room and beckoned me into her dark, cozy, smoky office.

She was a short, solid, sweet-faced woman with a graying braid wrapped around her head, Tyrolean style. It was months before I was able to retrieve the image that the sight of her evoked; finally I realized she looked like a composite of the "wives" from my illustrated Grimm's fairy tales—the woodcutter's wife, the fisherman's wife, the tinker's wife, a woman rendered in different costumes and settings but always with the same rosy, dimpled, soft-cheeked face. This was the kindly woman who opened the door of the thatched cottage to the lost brother and sister, willing to shelter them for the night but unable to break the spell that had set them on their wandering course, a weak but well-intentioned representative of the reality principle in the land of make-believe.

The silence in Dr. H's office was nearly as absolute as the silence in Dr. V's, but its tonal coloration was very different. I felt far more comfortable here, partly because I was now a veteran of what I understood to be psychoanalysis and I knew the drill: You came in, you lay down, you got up again when prompted at the end of the hour, and anything else was optional. But I also felt at home in this little cluttered basement room, where boxes of files were heaped in corners and books were piled knee-high around Dr. H's sagging chenille-covered armchair. I was in the presence of a fellow slob, and I liked that, but even more I liked the feeling of huddling in a warm untidy nest underground, a kind of spiritual root cellar.

Dr. H's knitting project got under way a few months after I began to come to her office. One day she startled me by following me to the couch. Before I had a chance to recline, she sat down next to me and presented me with a book of sweater patterns. Choose something, she said, in her flat midwestern accent; I'd like to knit a sweater for you, and when I peered at her incredulously, she smiled and nodded reassuringly. I flipped through the pages of the book, casting quick side-glances in her direction. Her proximity made me nervous and a little queasy; I was conscious of her wheezy breathing, and even though I lived with smokers, and was becoming a part-time smoker myself, I noticed the staleness of the odor that rose from her clothes. I looked through the book unseeingly—how could the world inhabited by these willowy models in cardigans and pullovers, posed with a cat in a window seat, or eating an apple while reading a book, have any connection to mine? — and made an impulsive, near-random choice. This one, I said, and simultaneously I was overcome with embarrassment at the certain knowledge that with its braided cables and mock turtleneck, that sweater was one of the most difficult to execute in the book. Dr. H dog-eared the page and handed me a box of yarn swatches. The color I chose came from the palette of the Rouault king in her waiting room — somehow the image of that painting stays with me more vividly than anything else I can remember from the Washington years — a brassy dark yellow.

Before I had a chance to object, Dr. H quickly and deftly measured me, across the shoulders and from shoulder to wrist. By the end of our next meeting she had produced a square of sweater the size of a placemat, and her needles worked steadily through the sessions. Given what I could see of her daily production rate, it seemed strange that the sweater grew so slowly over the weeks and months of my therapy: Was it possible that she unraveled it after hours, like Penelope? And what about her other patients? Did she keep a bag of knitting for each one of them as well, or was I somehow a special case?

I began to look forward to these restful sessions; in the half-lit quiet, my thoughts ordered themselves around the aural focal point of Dr. H's softly click-clacking needles. After a few months I became an adept of sorts; moments after I hit the couch, I was able to lower myself into a state of deep relaxation, fully alert but so heavy-limbed that I felt paralyzed. I saw myself as resting in a shallow bath of reverie, like a fish gently poaching in my mother's *bain-marie*, in liquid "barely to cover."

※   ※   ※

When my therapy with Dr. H ended in the spring—why it stopped I had no idea; I could only guess it was because the sweater was finished—she presented it to me. It was very handsome and unbecoming and smelled ever after of Dr. H's Pall Malls.

The following fall I was sent back to Williamstown to boarding school. My parents never mentioned it, but I knew that Dr. H had advised them to get me out of public school. I had felt the presence of her unseen hand earlier that winter, when the school bureaucracy caught up with my frequent absences. My parents' reaction to the note from the principal was eerily muted and nonjudgmental; even my father held his tongue. I could see now that, among other things, therapy could always be used as a retreat, a punishment-free zone.

It was an odd sensation to be sent home to school. I think perhaps my mother was acting on a primitive wish that the town might continue to protect me as it had when I was small. But the school sat up on a hill at the end of a long and unfamiliar driveway; I felt as far removed there from the scenes of my early childhood as I would have felt in Washington—farther perhaps, because physical proximity only seemed to sharpen the sense of temporal distance. On the few occasions when I got a chance to walk along College Place, I saw a new and unfamiliar pack of faculty brats running and shouting through the yards. The two houses in which I had spent my early childhood looked sturdily unchanged, and they seemed to stand away, regarding me with an air of innocent reproach.

Flagstone School was small and progressive, co-directed by the wealthy and eccentric Mrs. R, then in her seventies, and Ned, a man in his forties with a bulbous nose and a habit of wearing Harris tweeds, a cultivated Anglophile whose brusquely cheerful manner masked a complex and difficult personality. The school had a vague local reputation for oddness. It was housed in an old Italianate stucco manse with big airy rooms on the upper floors where female students lived in groups of five and six. The boys were kept in a converted barn down the hill at the end of a long path.

I can remember by heart many passages from my first Flagstone "report letter" (no grades were given). Ned wrote a kind of preamble, and even then I could see that he took pleasure in exercising his prose style, and also in the sense that he had "discovered" me. "I must confess to finding Emily a pure delight," he began, going on to describe my immaturity, my habit of wearing my clothes inside out, my "intensity"—"for Emily is *very* intense"—my "remarkable mind," and my ongoing failure to realize its potential. He also mentioned my tendency, when not sure of my facts, to "bull" my way through class discussion. I wasn't quite sure what to make of the arch tone of this assessment, its disconcerting combination of fulsome praise and campy disparagement, but I felt quite sure that it would please my mother, and it did.

My two years at Flagstone were relatively happy; I made friends, improved academically, and found a patient and attentive personal adviser in my elderly French teacher, Mr. Sears, who listened to me talk for half an hour every Saturday morning in a quiet corner of the teacher's smoking room. My roommates gave me a few blunt lessons in personal hygiene.

By trading on my quick tongue and my flair for imitations, I even achieved a measure of popularity. But I was also repeatedly caught in rules infractions—smoking in unsanctioned areas and sneaking off campus. Once I accepted a dare from my roommates to meet a Williams student, a Ugandan, in the basement of Lehman Hall, where I used to climb the fire escape as a child.

This man was in his thirties; he owned a coffee plantation in his native country; he had several wives and many children. His eyes were rheumy, and his fingers were cool and rough, like snakeskin. He carried a paper bag containing two cans of Budweiser and a pint of gin to our meeting place among the stained mattresses and dented file cabinets, and showed me the trick of pouring a little gin into the shallow rim of the can and sipping the beer through it.

My roommates had secreted themselves just outside the basement's rear entrance. When the Ugandan student heard their incompetently suppressed giggles and realized he had been set up, he burst into an indignant tirade, surely as much an expression of his disappointed loneliness and cultural dislocation as anything else. Under cover of that explosion I shot out of the basement and ran, followed by my roommates, all of us laughing and gasping for breath, until we collapsed in high grass behind the college library.

I worked the incident into a comic routine, rendering the Ugandan's outburst in Oxbridge-accented burp-talk. This was overheard by a faculty member, or perhaps another student informed on me. In any event, the story was extracted from me, and I was suspended for a week, a punishment far less severe than the sad, surprised look in Mr. Sears's eyes when we met for our weekly talk. Soon after my return to school, my roommates and I were caught smoking on the roof, and I was expelled. Why was I the one to be singled out, I asked Ned and Mrs. R as I stood before them in the firelit, wood-paneled faculty lounge. Why me and not my roommates, who in every case had been equally guilty? The explanation: Tricia and Caroline had come to Flagstone as shy and overly conscientious girls for whom a little wild behavior actually represented a developmental step *toward* maturity, rather than away from it. In their case it was appropriate for the school administration to look the other way.

*   *   *

By the time I was thrown out of Flagstone, my sister had gone away to college, and my parents had made the move to official Washington; now they and my brother lived in the embassy district in a townhouse where they were able to entertain on a large scale. This house was stringently vertical, stifling in summer and unevenly heated in winter. The first of its four floors was a tiled entryway; on the second my parents entertained guests. New and alienatingly formal furnishings came to rest in the living room—a pair of sofas upholstered in beige velvet, matching club chairs, small glass-and-rattan-topped tables, two grim brass urns flanking the fireplace, filled with silk flowers and gilt seed-pods, a tall Japanese screen painted with long-legged, pink-eyed water birds in black and gold. My family lived on the third and fourth floors; this was where the familiar and comfortable odds and ends of Williamstown furniture were kept.

Many times I came home at dinnertime to find a hired man in a starched white shirt and black vest stationed at the door. I got used to making my sullen and embarrassed way through the rustling, fragrant ranks of a crowd of strangers, my mother calling out, "You remember Emmy, don't you?" I learned to grab handfuls of hors d'oeuvres to take with me to my room on the fourth floor; the route to the kitchen was always blocked by knots of jabbering guests, and even if I made the effort to reach it, I knew I would find it taken over by an occupying army of caterers.

My mother enrolled me in the Edgar Allen Poe School. This was an extraordinary institution, exponentially weirder than Flagstone. It was housed in a soon-to-be-condemned Victorian house in northwest Washington, surrounded by an overgrown yard strewn with cigarette butts and broken glass. The directors were Alex O. and his wife, a visionary named Dorothy.

Alex was the front man; in spite of a missing molar that was apparent only when he smiled, he was presentable, and he gave off a reassuringly Ivy League air. Dorothy was the moving spirit of the place. I can see her now, a former field hockey star and debutante, a stocky woman in her late thirties with a rolling, athletic walk, making her way through the narrow halls of the school, her squarish, slightly trembling hands wrapped tightly around a coffee mug. She wore a soiled trench coat and penny loafers without socks; her scanty hair was pulled back tightly into a greasy ponytail. Her face—it can best be described as a slightly feminized version of William F. Buckley, Jr.'s; she had the same pinched nostrils and blazing blue eyes— was perpetually alight with enthusiasm.

When my mother and I arrived for my interview, we stepped over and around several installments of a dead crow on the front sidewalk. My mother must have been appalled by the condition of the school and by the condition of Dorothy as well, but placement had become a problem; there were few schools that would have me now.

But soon it was apparent that Poe would, because in her hoarse, whispery voice, Dorothy immediately launched into a sales pitch. The Poe school was not a conventional kind of place, she told us, nor was it a loose Summerhillian experiment. It was a rigorous academic environment where kids of all kinds were exposed, perhaps for the first time, to real intellectual inquiry. She and Alex and the staff worked very hard to give the kids the opportunity to learn in new, fresh ways. They did their best to help kids UNLEARN (as she warmed to her recruiting task, she began to speak in capitalized words and phrases) the old, stale lessons of the pedagogical past. On any given day, she said, throwing her arms out in an all-encompassing gesture, all kinds of EXCITING THINGS were going on around the school. Kids were learning about PYTHAGOREAN HAR-MONICS; kids were studying PLATONIC DIALOGUES. I was interested in poetry? In literature? Well, it JUST SO HAPPENED that one of the kids was the son of a poet with a national reputation who had agreed to take a position as poet-in-residence at the school. She had a hunch that I was EXACTLY THE KIND OF KID who would really BURST INTO BLOOM at Poe.

I glanced at my mother and saw that in spite of herself, she was impressed. Sophisticated though she was, there was still something of the credulous clubwoman in my mother, something of her own mother, and this part of my mother was looking at Dorothy and struggling to see past the blackened fingernails and unshaven legs, to look beyond these appearances to the devoted educator, so passionately committed that she had little time for personal grooming. And of course, my mother was also wishing that I might, as Dorothy promised, "burst into bloom." Even now it causes me some pain to admit that however remote my mother became, she never stopped suffering on my behalf.

I stayed at Poe for three years, repeating tenth grade. I soon found my place among the large group of students whose parents used Poe as a sort of loose corral, without much hope that their children would learn anything. I dropped in on classes that interested me—I was intrigued by Dorothy's course in the pre-Socratics—but I spent most of my time smoking in the weed-choked courtyard with a large group of fellow truants-in-residence. Sometimes Alex, whose daily job was to police the school and eject interlopers, would step out of his office and order us inside, but not often.

What I managed not to learn in high school sits firmly atop the foundation of what I had managed not to learn in junior high and elementary school. Taken together, it makes an impressive syllabus:

I never learned math beyond simple fractions, never learned geography, never learned history or any science beyond my sampling of the pre-Socratics and (a little) biology. I never learned about the branches of government, or grammar—though my usage is fairly correct. I learned a number of French words but never to conjugate verbs. My only real and continuous education consisted in the reading I did on my own; I read most of the contemporary favorites of the time—writers like Hesse and Salinger and Tolkien—and I also managed to acquaint myself with Jane Austen and George Eliot and Turgenev and Dostoyevsky, and Ezra Pound, T. S. Eliot, and some of the postwar American poets.

As an adult, I've spent a lot of anxious energy steering conversations around the holes in my general knowledge. Until I was well into my thirties, for example, it never occurred to me to examine my assumption that the Belgian Congo was located in Belgium. I was in my forties when I noticed that on a map, north is up and south is down. I've been enrolled almost continuously in undergraduate and graduate college programs, but I never retain much; whatever I pour into myself seems to leak out, leaving deposits of passive knowledge that I can't bring to consciousness with any reliability. In the past ten years, when I've begun to write in earnest, I've discovered that for me the key to retrieval is writing. But even this is outside the realm of my will; in the turbulence of composition, words and facts and paragraphs of quotation that I don't remember ever having learned come swirling up spontaneously into my consciousness.

Something about my brain is nonstandard; I seem to be good at thinking but bad at learning. Is it possible that in some cases thinking is inimical to learning? I don't blame my parents or my teachers for the failure of my education, and I can't entirely blame myself either, though I know I was lazy as well as learning-disabled. But I do blame Dorothy for summoning me to her office and subjecting me to harangues about my "centerlessness" and my "fundamental indecency." She and Alex were disgusted with me, she said, fed up, on the verge of throwing me out. I knew this was a hollow threat—no tuition-paying student was ever thrown out of Poe. The school was in desperate financial shape; unpaid teachers were lining up to sue the Os.

I learned that the only way to break the back of her frantic indignation was to begin to cry; at this point she would make the longed-for rhetorical turn, acknowledge that we'd reached bedrock and that perhaps I could now pick myself up and make another effort. She would clap her square hand onto my shoulder and walk me out of her office, pausing in the doorway to look up at me—she was rather short—with a tremulous smile. This was my cue to declare my good intentions and to be released.

On the afternoon that Kennedy was assassinated, school was dismissed early. I came home to the bewildering sight of my father, who never left his office in the middle of the day, standing on the sidewalk in his shirtsleeves and stocking feet. Tears were coursing down his face, and he was clutching my brother, who had just arrived home himself, to his chest. This was the first time I had ever seen him weep.

Obviously he had been waiting for us, looking to offer comfort or to receive it. As I approached, he beckoned and extended an arm. He pulled me to him and got my head into a kind of half nelson, pressing me against the half of his unfamiliar chest that wasn't occupied by Andy. He was vibrating with sobs, and I noticed that Andy, always loyal and good-hearted, was crying softly too. I found I could not respond to my father's embrace, and I allowed my arms to hang limply while I breathed through my mouth to avoid his scent, which was like the resinous deposit on the bowls of his pipes.

Not even for the thirty seconds that this three-way clinch lasted could I keep my thoughts from returning to the school courtyard where I had been sitting in the high grass just before voices began shouting the news from Dallas. I had been reading a poem a boy had handed me a few minutes earlier. One quick furtive skim had already shown me that this poem had nothing to do with me or love or anything immediately gratifying, but the distinction of having being asked to read it was enough to send me into physiological overdrive. My heart was banging; perspiration trickled down my inner arms. On a first reading I found the poem obscure; already I was running through possible responses—could I register some kind of appreciation without betraying my lack of understanding?

I was nearly sixteen now, and Eros had me in his grip. I was still hefty, but I had lengthened, and on my best days I managed to stay on the right side of the line that divides the attractive from the unfortunate. I had grown my hair long, and I washed and ironed it every morning; by noon my scalp had generated enough oil to turn my bangs into vision-impairing spikes. My days were full of sweaty lyricism; I had begun to leave Poe at lunchtime to spend my afternoons at Dupont Circle, where bongos and flutes were played under the trees and improvisational dances were performed.

On New Year's Eve, a few months after Kennedy's assassination, I was dragged out of an unauthorized and unchaperoned party by my father. At two o'clock in the morning, he tracked me to a house in suburban Maryland and found me with a boy—the same one who had given me the poem. This boy and I had been sitting on a washing machine in a darkened utility room, kissing and groping one another when my father burst in and pulled me away.

"Hey!" shouted the boy. "Wait a minute!" But my father was already frog-marching me through the rooms of the party, which emptied as we advanced. When we reached the front door, I made an attempt to wrestle myself free, but my father pushed me to the ground and dragged me by one ankle down the gravel driveway to the car. This was the first time my father had ever been physically rough with me (and the last). I was shrieking; my skirt was rucked up around my waist, exposing my underpants, and I felt a magnificent explosion of outrage and vindication in my chest. I was right, I told myself. I was innocent and good and finally this thing was happening that would prove I always had been.

He gathered me up and heaved me into the backseat. My mother sat silently in the front. I rolled onto the car floor—I was seriously drunk, and so, I would guess, was my father—where I lay mumbling, "I hate you, I hate you, I hate you." When my parents had gotten me home, my mother examined my gravel-scraped leg and ran a bath for me. While she was out of the bathroom for a moment, I broke a jar of aspirin in the sink, and in a rapture of anger I took a shard of glass and scratched my wrist hard enough to draw a little blood.

Everything about Dr. G's office breathed legitimacy—the boxy red brick building that housed it, the two big windows looking out across Connecticut Avenue to the trees of the Washington Zoo, the two armchairs that sat in the light of those windows, facing one another at a comfortable angle across a small oriental rug, the discreet placement of the analytic couch some yards away, the bookshelves lined with bound professional journals. Everything was airy and orderly, and standing in this room for the first time I found myself revising my views of Drs. V and H. They were part of an older tradition, I realized, not of the mainstream. Like the sightless clam that feels the sea floor with its retractable foot, I was beginning to learn some of the parameters of the therapy world.

What I realized instantly when Dr. G stood facing me in his waiting room, looking into my eyes with his sober, clear-eyed gaze, was that we had met before. Apparently he had failed to remember, but just a few weeks before our first session I had been in his house. That, in fact, was where the New Year's Eve that ended with the explosion had begun.

Dr. G and his wife were the hosts of an Italian exchange student who attended my school, a well-behaved and very European girl called Mimi (and what must she have made of Poe and Dorothy?). This Mimi, who was a good student with independent intellectual interests, had invited me and some others to a small New Year's Eve gathering.

I saw right away that this was a dull party; the guests had been drawn mostly from the small group of academic self-starters who followed Dorothy as she trucked through the halls of the school conducting ambulatory seminars. These were the kids who had incorporated her characteristic phrases into their own vocabularies, who spoke of "making order of the chaos of our sense perceptions" and "seeing it new." Only a few members of my wilder set were there, and we rolled our eyes at one another ironically; an exchange student like Mimi could hardly be expected to understand the gaffe she had committed by inviting us to a gathering of Dorothy devotees.

In the background, an Edith Piaf record played softly. We sat around a flagstone fireplace drinking mulled cider and eating Italian

Christmas cookies that I found austerely undersweetened. Mrs. G was a warm, sponsoring presence at Mimi's elbow, helping her with her English idioms and drawing out some of the shyer guests. I was itching to be gone, anxious to catch up with the larger group that I knew was even now guzzling Colt 45 malt liquor in some suburban rec room or on the towpath of the C&O canal. I was sufficiently addicted to smoking by now to feel pangs of nicotine withdrawal after half an hour of forced abstinence.

I had just begun to maneuver myself toward the door and the two friends who had stationed themselves there, ready to make their escape, when the man I was later to know as Dr. G leaned into the room. He was wearing a tan corduroy shirt and leather slippers. A pair of half-glasses rested on his nose, and a section of the *New York Times* was tucked under his elbow. "Ah," said Mimi, turning to him with a delighted smile. "Let me introduce . . ." and she carefully pronounced each of our names, first and last, while Dr. G moved around the room shaking hands, a weary, relaxed professional man at home. Having greeted the guests, he withdrew, but not before pausing at the threshold of the room to wish everyone a Happy New Year.

Moments later my two friends and I were packed into the front seat of a station wagon, lighting our cigarettes, driving toward Bethesda and the real party. Now the evening was over, and the night of cascading migrations from house to snowy-roofed suburban house, empty of parents, softly blinking with blue Christmas lights and thudding with rock-'n'-roll bass, had begun.

I never told Dr. G that I had been in his home. The fifteen seconds in which I might have spontaneously blurted out that information was already past when I rose from my chair in the waiting room to follow him into his office. What first blocked my impulse to be truthful was terror of my own clumsiness, the agony of self-disgust I knew I would suffer if my blundering candor embarrassed Dr. G or put him on the spot. Many years and several therapists later, I was to be initiated into the elaborate cordoning-off and sanitizing rituals that follow the acknowledgment of an "extra-analytic contact," but even as a psychoanalytic novice I understood that a glimpse of my therapist outside of his office represented the violation of a taboo. My invasion of Dr. G's home seemed an almost obscene transgression.

When we were seated he spoke. I gather there are some problems at home, he said. After a moment spent registering the twin novelties of sitting upright and being openly addressed, I said yes, my father had gotten very angry at me. I braced myself for the questions about particulars I assumed would follow. I was young enough to assume that I would be required to confess all the details of the make-out session my father had interrupted, and to feel mortified at the prospect. I was also anticipating the problem of what I would say if Dr. G demanded an account of the evening's beginning; I made a provisional plan to blur the details with vagueness and to resort to a lie only if pressed.

But Dr. G took another tack. I'm going to ask you some questions that I ask every new patient, he said, and he read rapidly through a medical/psychological checklist. Did I suffer from frequent stomach pain? Headaches? Sleeplessness? Was I, on a regular basis, a little bit sad? Somewhat sad? Very sad? Did I experience hallucinations? Did I believe enemies were trying to harm me? Did I hear voices? No. No. No. Somewhat. No. No. No. These were easy questions, and I was beginning to be lulled by the perfunctory tone in which Dr. G was reading them off. But toward the end of the list came one to give me pause: Had I ever tried to commit suicide? I asked myself: Could my wrist scratching count as an attempt at suicide? I half wished that it might, because suicide had a transcendent glamour that might redeem the squalid scene with my father I had apparently been excused from describing, at least for the moment. If I had made a suicide attempt, then I was a person in pain, a person whose pain had not been acknowledged, not been taken seriously, and I liked that prospect very much. But was there a risk that it might be taken *too* seriously?

I hedged. Sort of, I said, and Dr. G shot me a keenly inquiring look. I'm not sure if it really was, I said, and I went on to describe the episode, which I half assumed my mother had already told him about. (And perhaps, it occurred to me, she had, and Dr. G was feigning ignorance in order to elicit as much of the story from me as he could.) Dr. G put his clipboard aside and reached for a notebook. I found myself slowing the pace of my speech, as if I were dictating this maundering account to a secretary. Eventually I ground to a confused halt, and sat in silence while Dr. G completed his notes.

He looked up once again, and it seemed we were on to something else. How about school? he asked. How are things going there? Not so great, I said, with a self-conscious smile and a self-deprecating shrug. You seem bright, said Dr. G. You test bright. What do you think is the problem?

I tested bright. This could only mean that what I had vaguely feared for years was true. That blue folder resting on Dr. G's chairside table, under his small hand with its slender curled fingers and thick white-gold wedding band—I felt sure it contained the results of the tests the psychologist in North Adams had administered to me when I was eight. These numbers had been following me from therapist to therapist, and this meant that my suspicions had been accurate, that the silent ladies, Drs. V and H, had known things about me that I never knew about myself.

On the other hand, if I tested bright, this meant I *was* bright. I had been tried, and found not to be wanting. The chill I had felt at the sight of the blue folder became a suffusion of warmth, and I saw the object as an almost magically powerful talisman. I looked at the bound volumes on Dr. G's shelves, and it seemed almost plausible that the contents of the blue folder might be incorporated into a sympathetic article somewhere in those pages: Emily Gordon, it would begin, a young girl with a high IQ and troubles at home, was seen in the offices of Dr. G . . .

My sister owns a photograph of my father and President Johnson in Johnson's office at the Johnson ranch in Texas, taken in 1964 over the Christmas holiday. The president is wearing jeans and a flannel shirt. His feet, in cowboy boots, are propped on his desk. He is squinting fiercely at a document of some kind, and my father, by then director of the budget, is standing on one side of the desk in profile, wearing a dark suit and a tie, looking characteristically exhausted and uncharacteristically deferential.

That great prosthetic memory, the Internet, has retrieved for me an article from the July 24, 1964, issue of *Time* magazine. Under the heading "More Tightfisted," my father is described as having "quietly emerged as one of Washington's rising powers" and as a man who "already has more personal contact with Johnson than anyone outside of his inner staff." My father's close relationship with Johnson, said *Time*, "developed within 24 hours of the Kennedy assassination when the matter of finishing up the fiscal 1965 budget was pressing." My father and the president worked together for what

Time quotes Johnson as calling (rather mythopoeically) "thirty-seven days and nights."

I was too self-absorbed to have registered any of this at the time, but now I can't help finding it striking that those thirty-seven days and nights fell between November 3 and December 31. This information supports my sense that immediately after his startling collapse into tears on the news of Kennedy's death, my father disappeared into the Washington maw for good. Only in moments of extremity—and his behavior that New Year's Eve, I can see now, must have been influenced by the accumulated strain of those thirty-seven days—did he reveal anything more than glimpses of his subjectivity.

In Williamstown the cocktail hour had been observed casually and intermittently—a drink or two in the kitchen while children flowed in and out with questions to be answered and disputes to be resolved. In Washington it evolved into an institution. Every night when my father was home for dinner, it was convened in the upstairs living room, across the carpeted landing from my parents' large chilly bedroom with its high double windows that looked out across Wyoming Avenue into a similar set of windows on the third floor of the Kuwaiti embassy. My mother carried a tray up from the kitchen, laden with two squat, heavy-bottomed old-fashioned glasses filled with ice, a bowl of raw vegetables, and a smaller bowl of kosher salt in which to dip them. Sometimes the tray also held cheese and crackers or a tub of my mother's chicken liver pâté, but these additions grew rarer after my father was discovered to have high cholesterol. My father poured the drinks—bourbon for him, a martini for her—out of bottles kept in a small antique wooden cabinet my mother had stripped and refinished years earlier in Williamstown.

My mother excused herself after half an hour to attend to dinner. My father measured another jigger and a half of bourbon into his glass and settled down to read the paper and watch the news. Downstairs in the kitchen, my mother replenished her drink, but she poured freehand, and by the time we all sat down at the table she was often quite drunk. This was nothing subtle; she swayed in her chair, missed the glass when she poured herself wine. My brother and I did our best to ignore these symptoms and to hope that on this evening the moment wouldn't arrive when my father would sigh harshly and rise to his feet, hoist my mother out of her chair, and help her up the stairs, where he would leave her propped on her chaise longue with a blanket over her knees, then retire to his study, to work at his desk until eleven.

I made a point of arriving for my appointments with Dr. G exactly on time. On the few occasions when I got there five minutes early, I invariably walked into the waiting room to encounter my classmate Tamara Federman, the fat blinking girl with the bald spot, being dismissed from her session. I once caught a glimpse of Dr. G, standing halfway between his chair and the partially open door, waiting for Tamara to disappear from view before closing it, looking blank but alert, like an empty cruising cab with its on-duty sign lit.

Tamara's parents were Eastern Europeans of some kind—it was typical of my general incuriosity that I never wondered which country they came from—and she spoke with a faint accent. She was miserably shy; at lunchtime she sat by herself in a corner of the courtyard, hunched over a brisket sandwich, her jaws working steadily and her eyes darting furtively. Once, the legend went, a group of boys got into her locker before lunch and substituted a dead bird for the meat in her sandwich. I lowered my eyes as she walked through the waiting room; to acknowledge that I shared Dr. G with Tamara would be to risk undoing all the efforts I had made to pass for a plausible sixteen-year-old girl.

I was nearly as uncomfortable about my failure to mention Tamara to Dr. G as I had been about my failure to mention the fact of my presence in his house. I saw that I was shirking my responsibility as a patient; by then I was beginning to understand that to make these kinds of disclosures and to examine their meaning would amount to working through resistance—the essential metabolic process of psychotherapy.

What I never acknowledged to myself as I fixed on the withholding of those two pieces of information was that I had also made many other, far more significant omissions. I never told Dr. G, for example, that over the months my mother was drinking more steadily and in greater quantities; that she was drunk at dinner nearly every night, even on those increasingly frequent ones when my father was not at home and there was no cocktail hour to provide cover for her drinking; that Andy and I sat through meals in silent bewilderment as she poked ineffectually at her plate, her fork deployed at an awkward flat angle that made it impossible to spear food efficiently, then gave up on eating altogether, pushed her plate away, and fumblingly lit a cigarette.

I never told him how behavior that once had been episodic was now nearly constant; my mother increasingly was spending her days as a semirecluse, lying on the chaise in her bedroom. I sometimes heard her coughing as I passed her door on my way up the stairs to my room. "Come in," she would call out softly when I knocked, and I would find her reclining in a pool of lamplight, her Peter De Vries novel open on her lap, smiling mistily and holding out an affectionate hand, greeting me with an odd, theatrical air of fond recognition, as if I had just arrived from a great distance to visit her.

I also never told him about my father's peculiar blinkered way of dealing with my mother's slow-motion collapse—how one night, for example, he encountered me on the stair landing and gestured me into his study. "Look," he whispered, opening his jacket to reveal a paper bag full of my mother's prescription medications. "I'm going to keep these in here for a while," he said, "just to be on the safe side." I stood and watched, speechless with confusion and astonishment, while my father stashed the bag in the back of his file drawer. This dissociated craftiness seemed so unlike my formidably rational father, so out of touch with what he must have believed to be the seriousness of the situation. Was my mother addicted to these pills? Was she suicidal? And if so, were these matters to be handled in such a childish way? And why me? My father rarely even spoke to me anymore. Why was I the one chosen for the wink and nudge?

Why did I omit to mention any of this to Dr. G? Perhaps I was "in denial," as present-day conventional wisdom about the families of alcoholics would have it, but I don't think this explanation quite applies (though it fits my father's behavior quite neatly). I was very young then, and the world was younger too; I knew that therapy represented a punishment-free zone, but I hadn't yet come to the liberating realization that it was also an arena in which I could rat on my parents with impunity. Dr. G and my parents lived in the world of adults—that alone was enough to make them seem natural allies. And the atmosphere of Dr. G's office held a certain authority and clarity that I could not help associating with my father—both men could, after all, be loosely classified as social scientists.

I think also that I was responding to an imperative of adolescence, the self-preserving need to stay partially cocooned, to remain agnostic about things that as yet I lacked a frame of reference to understand, to push certain obtruding realities out of my way so that I could continue to grow—and by "grow" I mean literally to mature neurologically, to grow up. What *did* I talk about? Early on I talked about my boyfriend—I had recently fallen seriously in love for the first time, and I was subject to a constant incontinent urge to talk about it. Dr. G maintained an absolutely neutral demeanor while I went on about this boy and his brilliance and complexity. Eventually I began to realize that the air in the office went dead whenever I broached this subject. Even in his expressionless silence, Dr. G was sending me discouraging signals. Embarrassed, I fell silent again, spending most of the hour in mute fantasy—not a comfortable thing to do when sitting upright and facing a therapist, but not impossible for an adept like me.

In an apparent effort to jump-start the therapeutic process, Dr. G began to interrupt my reveries. This was a novelty, and not entirely a welcome one. I missed the restfulness of Dr. V's and Dr. H's offices, where the silence was principled and predictable. In Dr. G's office it was also the rule (except for the first few sessions, when he spoke more than he did in all the later ones put together), but one he allowed himself to override. The pressure to make progress—whatever that might mean—was stronger here; I could feel a certain masculine urgency here, a sense of being goosed along.

"So," he would say, after twenty minutes of silence had elapsed. Sometimes he would repeat the word—"So. So." Prompted, I would edge into the one topic that I felt sure he approved of, the disjunction between my intellectual potential and my school performance. A certain amount of dissimulation crept in here, because there was very little school performance at all in those days, and not much school attendance either. But I liked the topic, because I had found that by applying the word "lazy" to myself, I could compel Dr. G to defend me against my self-accusation. You are not lazy, he would insist, leaping out of his neutrality like a jack-in-the-box. Nobody is lazy. "Lazy" is nothing but a shorthand—a shorthand, I extrapolated, for a long chain of causality that had rendered me free of any responsibility.

One day, in passing and for the first time, I happened to mention a dream. Dr. G sat up smartly in his chair and reached for his clipboard. Tell me more, he said. He scribbled intently as I spoke, obviously anxious not to slow down or interrupt my account, looking up from his notes to give me quick, hyperalert glances.

The dream was one I had dreamed years earlier, when we first moved to Washington, and it was simple, memorable, and frightening. In the dream I was reading in bed. My mother came into the room to say good night to me. Put away the book and go to sleep, she said. She left and I turned off the light, but after a moment I turned it on and took up my book again, with a guilty consciousness that I was defying my mother's wishes. Suddenly the perspective of the dream shifted, and I found myself looking down on the roofs of Broxburn Court, our old suburban cul-de-sac, from a place high up in the night sky. The houses were lighted, and everything was still. I knew that in the moment when I had turned my light back on, sat up and opened the book, every human being in the world had disappeared, and that I was completely alone.

Like a laboratory pigeon pecking randomly at a panel of buttons, I had apparently hit the one that made seed mix come gushing out of the spout. When I finished my narration, I looked up to see that Dr. G had put down his clipboard and removed his half-glasses. My dream had obviously moved him; he was looking into my eyes with unguarded sympathy. For just a moment he had permitted himself to shrug off his professional disguise, relaxed into being the man I had seen in his home, in his slippers and corduroy shirt. This was the reward, the brass ring snatched and pocketed, and from this point on, the pace of my therapeutic education—which for five years had been shadowing my academic education—picked up sharply.

The moment passed; Dr. G acknowledged it with a regretful sigh, shuddering faintly on the exhale, as if he were calling himself back to his duties. What came to my mind in connection to the dream? he asked. What kind of book could it be that my mother had forbidden me to read, and why would reading it mean the end of the world?

As the months wore on, Dr. G's interjections grew rarer. Almost imperceptibly he had begun a weaning process: Each session he withdrew further into silence. It was that silence, or the breaches of it—ever more meaningful as they grew rarer—that taught me the topography of the therapy world.

What did I learn? A large part of the lesson was simply review. What I already knew was confirmed and underwritten: Almost anything I said would disappear into a pit of silent neutrality. My offerings were a long time falling, and they hit the distant bottom with the faintest of thuds. My hesitations in Dr. V's office had turned out to be well founded; Dr. G's impassivity confirmed my early suspicions that the events of my daily life were too humble and particular to serve as a fit topic for therapy. On more than one occasion I entered his office fighting tears because of some slight I had suffered at school and spent the hour staring fixedly at a place on the wall a few inches south of Dr. G's head. I knew better than to risk a collapse into blubbering when Dr. G would do nothing more consoling than to pass me the Kleenex.

But tears that welled up in response to the telling of a dream or a dimly remembered childhood event were warmly received. I had only to mention a dream to make Dr. G's face take color and expression. This transformation always made me think of a magic show I had attended as a child: The magician called a pretty girl onto the stage and presented her with a bouquet of tightly curled rosebuds. As she stood, blushing, doing her best to endure a barrage of impertinent questions from the magician, the roses she was cradling unconsciously in the crook of her elbow began to bloom, and simultaneously a great hum of gratified amazement from the audience began to grow.

Whenever I woke up remembering a dream, I carried it through the noise and distraction of my day at school like a fragile gift. More often than not, pieces of the dream melted and slid away in the hours of daylight; by late afternoon, when I sat down in my chair opposite Dr. G, half of it would be gone, and what remained would be incoherent. I freely reconstructed missing details, and on a few occasions replaced a wholly vanished dream with an invented one. But I did so with trepidation; it seemed to me that dreams, like paper currency, might be made of material with a distinctive weave, and that a dream maven like Dr. G might well recognize a counterfeit.

Freshly unearthed memories were prized even more highly than dreams. It was in Dr. G's office that I first told the story about the giant egg that Andy and I had collaborated in drawing on the wall of our bedroom with our crayons. I presented this as a recently dredged-up discovery, but in fact it was not only a well-established memory but also a frequently repeated family story, one of my mother's favorites. Dr. G took the bait; he was scribbling as I spoke, shaking his head in amazed delight.

It was not long before I began to feel I was sitting in a pocket of fraudulent stench. My omissions, exaggerations, and fabrications had been piling steadily up, but what really troubled me was the discontinuity between the sensitive and vulnerable self I presented to Dr. G and the self that lived outside the office, the self that laughed loudly, ate greedily, debated volubly, and scoffed at offenses to its common sense. This two-self problem was recent; it had never bothered me when I was lying on the couches of Drs. V and H. In those days, I had still taken therapy for an exercise in make-believe; never for a moment had I confused myself with the infant I had been playing at. The difference now was that I had begun the task of integrating the parts of myself into a whole, and I found that I could not contain my contradictions.

Which self was I? This was a question I took seriously. In my mind the dilemma seemed as urgent and foundational as the questions of the pre-Socratics. What stuff is the world made of? Dorothy would ask this as she paced the front of the classroom. Is it characterized by unchanging stillness or by ceaseless flux? Is it one or is it many?

As I continued in therapy with Dr. G, I began to tilt radically toward the vulnerable side of the opposition. My guilt about the deceptions and manipulations I had practiced in his office propelled me in that direction, as did the belief—very much part of the era's zeitgeist—that passivity and vulnerability were more attractive than rude health. But there were also deeper motivating reasons: Like anyone growing up in the 1960s, I believed that authenticity was the first and only virtue, and I had learned by now to locate what was authentic in myself as lying close to unconsciousness.

I felt the powerful reductive suction of psychoanalytic thinking. My years of psychotherapy had taught me to move away from
the future toward the past, away from the cognitive toward the
emotional, away from the complex toward the simple, away from
the sophisticated toward the primitive, away from the active and
toward the passive—away from the world and toward the self.

*   *   *

The summer before I turned eighteen I spent living with my
boyfriend in a series of borrowed apartments. In August, he and I
took the train to Indianapolis, where we stayed with his thrice-
divorced mother for a few weeks, after which he left to go to college in Vermont and I returned to Washington. I had no college
plans, so I moved back into my parents' house. For a few months
we achieved a fragile rapprochement.

My mother had taken a job teaching at a small, expensive private school in suburban Maryland, and she managed to find a
teacher's-aide position there for me. We drove the long commute
together in companionable silence. I began to join my parents for
the cocktail hour—they allowed me a glass of sherry, sometimes
two. I helped my mother cook. She seemed more stable now that
she had work to do outside the house, and while she continued to
drink, she drank less. Sometimes I watched the news with my
father; at the dinner table I began to engage him in political discussions. I continued to see Dr. G.

In December my boyfriend returned to Washington for the
Christmas break, and the two of us took the train to Indianapolis
once again. After a few weeks, he went back to college in Vermont,
but I stayed on for another month. When he wrote me a letter telling
me he had fallen in love with someone else, I responded by scratch-

ing at my wrists with a pair of nail scissors. The boyfriend's mother put me on the train back to Washington.

The day after my return, my parents took me to Dr. G's office. When the three of us were ushered into the room, I knew immediately that my therapy was over. Some membrane had been punctured; the office was contaminated. Two unfamiliar folding chairs had been produced for my parents to sit in — chairs that, I supposed, had been lurking in Dr. G's small utility closet all along.

It had already been decided — when and by whom I never knew and never asked to know — that I could no longer live at home. Dr. G presented us with two options: I could enter a pilot family therapy program for troubled adolescents at the National Institute for Mental Health in Bethesda, where I would live in a dormitory and my parents and siblings would come for twice-weekly sessions with a team of therapists.

Or I could go away to Austen Riggs. Dr. G described this as the traditional alternative, and to my mind it was far more alluring than the NIMH program, which sounded dismayingly clinical. I could imagine myself walking under the arcade of tall lilac bushes that I remembered from my visits to the Riggs campus; in my mind's eye I was transformed into a pale, attenuated, idealized version of myself, pensive and lovely and lost in dreaminess. On my forays with Caroline, I had been a grubby civilian, unbecomingly eager for a glance at the mysteries practiced in the Inn. As a patient, I would become one of the initiated.

Predictably, my father seemed to like the NIMH option. Was this program, he asked, regarded as respectable? Oh, entirely, said Dr. G. Otherwise NIMH would never give it houseroom. My father seemed open to the idea that this kind of directive, accelerated therapy might bring us all closer; it appealed to his problem-

solving, future-oriented cast of mind. And besides, it was sure to
be far less expensive than Austen Riggs. Almost immediately he
was sold on the proposal, eager to leave the office and get started.
Dr. G turned to my mother, who had remained silent through the
discussion. Every family member should be comfortable with a
decision like this, he said. How did she feel about it?

My mother paused for a moment, an ironic, lingering smile
playing at the corners of her mouth, and gave her verdict. She was
sure that the NIMH program represented the most up-to-date thinking in the profession, she said, and she was also sure that many people would find that kind of thing helpful, but she was too old-fashioned, too reticent, and perhaps just too selfish, to find it attractive.
She gave Dr. G her most rueful, most apologetic smile, got a small
acknowledging smile in return, then turned her smile on my father
and me. Is that all right, my dears? Can you forgive me for my cow-
ardice?

My father protested; Riggs was a place for the wealthy, he
argued. Even a stay of a few months would bankrupt us. Dr. G suggested that he look into the provisions of his government insurance
policy. It was just possible that some of the Riggs expenses might be
covered. When we got home that afternoon, my father went into his
study and made a few phone calls. He discovered that his insurance
would indeed cover the major part of the cost of a private hospitalization for at least a year, and that in the end Riggs might actually
cost us less than NIMH.

So Riggs it was. Arrangements were made, and the day before I
was to leave for Stockbridge, I met with Dr. G for a final session. The
atmosphere in the office was strikingly different; the therapeutic suction machine had been turned off, and both Dr. G and I were a little self-conscious in the absence of its steady, mesmerizing hum. We

spoke in alternating blurts, like strangers waiting at a bus stop. So, said Dr. G. This will be a change for you. Yes, I said, I guess it will be. A challenge too, he added. Yes, I said.

Just before we rose to our feet at the end of the hour, Dr. G smiled shyly, cleared his throat, and spoke. Do you know, he said, that I recently had a dream about you? Or more properly, he corrected, about his feelings of identification with me. This was the dream: He was back at Columbia as a brand-new freshman, wearing his beanie, late for his first class. His parents had simply dropped him off on Broadway, outside the gates of the university. Nobody had bothered to show him around, and he was wandering through the campus, lost.

5

A Serious Friend

*I*n the two years I spent as a Riggs outpatient, I learned some lessons, most of them negative. I learned that if I dumped my cotton India print dresses into the dryer at the laundromat, they would emerge child-sized. I learned that a phone bill left unpaid for months would cause my phone to go dead. I learned that my failure to pay my rent would result in a campaign of harassment by a character named Orren W. Champer, a one-man credit agency who wrote me letters in a spidery, nineteenth-century hand, chiding me for my negligence and assuring me that I was fundamentally a decent person whose conscience would eventually compel me to do the right thing. I learned that a broiler used repeatedly to grill lamb chops without being washed would burst into flames. I learned that a toothache should be brought to the attention of a dentist before waves of pain and pressure became unbearable. I learned that wearing the same pair of jeans every day for two weeks would make those jeans give off a powerful mushroom odor, even though I took daily showers. I learned all these things, but somehow I failed to take the step of putting my new knowledge into practice.

I started my outpatient career by sharing a railroad flat in Lenox, where the rents were cheaper than in Stockbridge. I shared these rooms with a nonpatient, a frugal, musical girl who wore thrift-store clothes and knew how to clean and cook. That arrangement ended when it occurred to some of my Riggs acquaintances that they could get around a recent alcohol ban at the Inn by using my apartment for extended binges.

I moved on to a semifurnished apartment immediately opposite the Riggs campus, owned by a Christian Scientist who showed up at the door for surprise inspections and expected the rent to be paid punctually. I lived there for a summer with the boyfriend who was later to get me pregnant, then for a few months with a new outpatient roommate, a melancholy, well brought-up Californian redhead named Karen, who sat cross-legged on the floor playing her accordion when in her cups. Like my earlier Lenox roommate, Karen was competent. She moved into the noisome summer mess the boyfriend and I had created, surveyed the rooms with a sigh, and proceeded to throw herself into heavy cleaning, pulling on rubber gloves and dragging a mess of semiliquefied sprouted onions from under the sink, then dousing the area with ammonia and scrubbing it clean with a hard-bristled brush specially purchased at the hardware store. She lined the kitchen shelves with self-adhesive paper and poured bleach down the drains, while I watched with interest and a faint dismay. Where had she learned to do all this? I wondered. How was it that other people absorbed practical knowledge so readily? How did one begin to learn to take care of oneself?

The landlord inspected the apartment with widened eyes and

a smile. His reaction made me proud and happy, though I had contributed little to the transformation. But soon he announced that he had decided to give this apartment to his married daughter, and once again I moved, this time to the second floor of a converted carriage house, a charming collection of rooms with tent ceilings and a big bay window. My roommates here were unwilling to clean up after me; they punished me by throwing all the clothes I had left strewn through the apartment out my bedroom window onto the driveway.

Like other Riggs outpatients, I struggled with a sense of exile. I ate at the Inn more frequently than the rules allowed and repeatedly risked banishment by furtively stuffing my backpack with popovers and chicken drumsticks wrapped inefficiently in napkins. When my apartment was too cluttered or filthy to be endured, too full of my roommates' noise or silence, I found myself moseying down Main Street toward the Inn, where the domestic staff emptied the ashtrays and the record player was kept in working order.

As an outpatient, I attended community meetings more regularly than I did when I lived in the Inn. I told myself that I showed up at these functions in order to gather anecdotes for my sessions with Dr. Farber, that the observations I made of the patients and staff would make it possible for me to work up new imitations for his amusement. But I was also drawn to them because my outpatient existence was so marginal and free-form that any regular daily event gave my life a shape. The presence of outpatients drew questions from the inpatients: Shouldn't we be making the transition to independent living? they asked. And wasn't our presence in these meetings and at meals a symptom of regression? After a certain number of these complaints had been lodged, Richard the protofacilitator could be relied upon to intervene. Okay, people, he would call out from his seat on the floor. What exactly are the boundaries of our community? Who is us and who isn't?

How difficult it is to abandon the ironic mode and speak enthusiastically! When I remember Dr. Farber at Riggs, the colors of his office spring back into my mind. I remember the Navajo rug on his floor—or was it hung on the wall?—a lively abstract design of triangles in turquoise blue, mustard yellow, red and black. I remember the ranks of books on his shelves and the two deep red leather chairs in which we sat. I remember Dr. Farber's small-chinned, delicate-boned face—a rather ugly face, to be honest, but a fascinating vehicle for expression.

My twice-a-week meetings with Dr. Farber were the heart of my existence as a Riggs outpatient. His full, rich, pungent, complex humanity was a revelation to me. The power of his presence jerked the world into focus; what had seemed pale and attenuated, blurred and mixed, jumped into clarity and bold relief. I remember the surprising verve of his walk and the elegant and efficient way he handled his keys when he let us into his office early on a Saturday morning, one eye squeezed shut against the cigarette in the corner of his mouth.

Both of us smoked continually as we talked, and as a hazy blue lozenge of tobacco smoke formed above our heads, and butts piled up in the commodious ceramic ashtrays he provided, Dr. Farber warmed to his subject, twisting himself into odd postures, flinging a leg over the arm of his chair.

What did we talk about? We talked about Dr. Farber's childhood in Douglas, Arizona—how being a westerner and a Jew growing up in a desert landscape as the eldest of three rivalrous and loving brothers had affected his view of the world. We talked about my child-

hood in Williamstown, and for the first time I began to see my history from a sociological point of view, to understand the advantages
of coming from an intellectually accomplished family, and also the
implicit discouragements—the sense that my parents had reserved
for themselves the hopes and ambitions that members of an earlier
generation might have passed on to their children. We talked about
his marriages and my boyfriends. We talked about his growing dismay at watching Riggs patients, most of them young and few really
sick, loitering in a psychiatric limbo.

We talked about the youth culture, which was then a relatively
new phenomenon. Dr. Farber found it fascinating. He was always
asking questions about its customs and mores, and I understood
myself to be his informant on these matters. I remember sitting in
a cabin in the South Egremont woods at three o'clock in the
morning, clustered around a potbellied stove with a group of hip-
pie trust-funders who lived communally there, several of them
quite naked in spite of the cold, passing a cigar-sized joint. I was
struggling to keep a log of the experience in my cannabis-addled
head, memorizing what there was of dialogue, relishing the
prospect of telling Dr. Farber all about it in the morning. How he
would enjoy the detail—I was sure—of the gold-stamped black
paper in which the marijuana had been rolled.

We talked about movies and TV. We spent one session dis-
cussing a patient, a tall young man with rumpled dark hair and a
slow, sad smile who stayed up most of the night in the small TV
viewing room in the bowels of the Inn. This was a source of worry to
his therapist, who felt that his patient was using television as a way to
hide from the world. (But what world, Farber remarked, was there at
Riggs to avoid?) This concern was aired in the young man's conference, and after the doctors had spent some minutes deploring the

regressive temptations of TV, Dr. Farber asked: What exactly was the patient watching? Old movies, I think, said the young man's therapist. Well, Dr. Farber quoted himself as answering, that seems entirely sensible to me. That's exactly what I'd spend *my* time doing if I were a patient at Riggs.

My own third staff conference came and went. Dr. Farber's report was brief and succinct: They made you sound like a little machine, he said. A little machine that could barely make it to the bathroom, he added.

And we continued to talk. We gossiped freely about both patients and staff. I brought him stories, for example, about Pat, perhaps the most vivid of the four or five Riggs patients who were actually crazy. She was an heiress, and someone had been unwise enough to allow her unlimited access to her money. She careened through the Berkshires buying cars, cosmetic surgery—feel my breasts! she was forever insisting—drugs, jewelry, exotic animals, the contents, sight unseen, of a warehouse full of antiques, and a Victorian mansion on a multiacre estate, in bad repair. She shoved the furniture into the house in random groupings, loaded the surfaces with blazing candelabra, and threw a party for Riggs patients, where she distributed prescription pills by the multicolored handful.

Pat was rail-thin and lantern-jawed. With her prominent collar bones, her pallor, and her bouffant blonde wigs, she looked like a cancer patient. She jittered, giggled, and talked obsessively, all with a jarring disregard for conversational rhythms. Her eyes were dazed and dead. Everyone, even the nurses, backed away from her approach.

Dr. Farber was never one to honor institutionally approved sanctimony. Ordinarily, he was quick to laugh at tales of lunacy, but on the particular day I'm remembering, he listened to my tale about

Pat—which I've since forgotten—with a faraway look, and when I came lamely to the end of it, he told his own story about Pat's aimless road trips in her vintage MG, during which she stuffed herself with Hershey bars and pills, veering over to the side of the road to vomit or pass out. I felt the smile fade from the corners of my mouth as I registered the tonal change in Dr. Farber's voice and the expression of puzzled sadness in his eyes. He was, I realized, being serious now.

I had grown up in a witty household. I had learned the rhythmical give-and-take of anecdote trading, and I was quick to return a serve. I knew this facility was one of the traits Dr. Farber found appealing in me, one of the reasons he had changed his mind and agreed to take me on as a patient. But the clever talk at my parents' dinner table was of a very rule-bound kind. The troubled compassion I heard in Dr. Farber's voice would have jarred and silenced my parents, and it stopped me cold.

I was beginning to understand that seriousness had always embarrassed my parents. Their compulsive anecdotalism, their puns and wordplay, even their custom of predinner drinking—all these were means by which they instinctively kept it at bay. Especially for my mother, it was imperative to view the world a little obliquely, and while she would allow sentiment, she would not allow seriousness. I must confess that I feel a little bewildered by it myself, a little at sea in what even now seems to me a perpetually new and recently discovered element.

Suddenly, in the midst of what I had taken to be a gossip and story-swapping session, Dr. Farber had given me a quick, vivid, indelible glimpse of his imaginative apprehension of madness— its monotony and loneliness, its terrifying perspectivelessness. But seriousness, I was beginning to see, was the source of all surprise and mystery, and here was just the kind of serious surprise that talk with Dr. Farber was full of. I never forgot it, and it cured me forever of my tendency to romanticize mental illness. Nothing, Farber once observed, is more boring than madness.

Perhaps it would be more precise to say that Dr. Farber gave me a glimpse of what lay at the limits of his imagination—madness resists the overtures of the imagination. It is the opacity of madness that makes it boring, and also makes it inaccessible to psychotherapy. Farber wrote memorably about the intractability of this problem in one of his essays, "Schizophrenia and the Mad Psychotherapist." He chronicled the long and passionately well-intended engagements of therapists with schizophrenics, concluding that the result of these therapeutic struggles is very often not an improvement in the patient but a deterioration in the doctor. Years of exposure to the impoverishment of language and imagination that characterize severe mental illness have their effect on the therapist, who often succumbs to the temptation to invest the silence or nonsense of the patient with oracular or prophetic significance. And soon enough the therapist begins to crave the crude and vivid melodrama, the compelling life of projection he has found in the company of schizophrenics, and he loses his tolerance for ordinary human mutuality. The mad psychotherapist can be identified by his addiction to gesture and his impatience with language. He becomes "an apostle of relation who can no longer abide relation."

For Farber, what Martin Buber called "imagining the real" was essential to all relation, and especially to the relation between therapist and patient. A further distinction in Farber's thinking was between imagining and knowing. His essays register appreciation as well as criticism of Freud, whom he describes as "one of the great imaginative geniuses of the age." But he also, and paradoxically, sees Freud as an enemy of the imagination, which he "warred continually against" and "equated with 'illusion.'" Freud's greatest heresy, in Farber's mind—and here was the item of his thinking that most directly influenced his unusual practice as a therapist—was his presumption that "one can, instead of imagining, know the other in his essence."

Farber anatomized the problematic connection between imagination and the will. It is precisely when imagination fails, as it did in the case of the mad psychotherapist, that the will rushes in to do— in Yeats's famous formulation—its work. Out of this perception sprang Farber's concept of the isolated will, and most of his early essays address the ways in which our culture betrays the workings of what he called "willfulness." Our frenetic efforts to will what cannot be willed—to penetrate what we cannot understand, for example, or to love what we cannot love—are the effects of living in what Farber called the era of the "disordered will."

Leslie Farber was a rigorous thinker, but not a systematic one. The notion of the will in his writings was not a world-flattening theoretical machine. It was more theme than thesis, a sinuous line that threaded its way through topically diverse essays. In his work, ideas were always firmly subjugated to his vision of life. He wrote essays of high literary quality in a prose dense with thought, but always accessible, and equally removed from both of the extremes that have come to characterize psychoanalytic writing— the jargon-clotted private language of the journals and the simple-minded list-form exhortations of the self-help popularizers.

Early in his career, Farber dealt with psychopathologies like schizophrenia and hysteria in terms of the isolated will, but later he moved away from these categories toward more general, often highly personal, ruminations about the human condition, particularly relations between men and women. By the time he was writing his late essays, the idea of the will was still informing his thinking, but it had been eclipsed by deepening preoccupations with mortality and human connection.

Reading his early work, one senses that he began as a collegial member of his profession. These essays reflect a firm identification with his fellow psychoanalysts, even if that identification was qualified by doubts about what he called the "prescientific" pretensions of the discipline. But later, as the implications of his views worked themselves out in his writing and his life, he seemed to move to a position of loyal opposition.

And still later, it began to seem that any faith he had in psychoanalysis had eroded to the vanishing point, and that he had grown disenchanted with the profession. The excesses of the 1960s had something to do with this, and also a darkening of mood and vision that was partly the result of ill health.

It was in my outpatient years at Riggs that I completed my first reading of Dr. Farber's essays. I read them slowly, with great care and some struggle, and I was deeply impressed by them. At this point he had published only ten, but each one was a small, hard-won essayistic masterpiece. In his portrait of the mad psychotherapist, I was delighted to recognize the Riggs director, with his cowboy boots, his mumbling speech, and his bevy of mad beauties. And although my knowledge of intellectual history was shot through with large holes of ignorance, I could sense the ancient provenance of Farber's preoccupation with the will. I was thrilled—almost shocked—to recognize some pre-Enlightenment notions in these essays, and to feel the presence of a religious radiance in their deepest recesses.

God! I remember thinking. Dr. Farber believes in God! Given

my upbringing, this was a source of titillation and alarm. I knew how closely he guarded his belief, how he kept it closed to all but the most serious inquiries, and I never dared to ask questions about it. I must confess that I've never really been able to understand his belief; the best I can say is that years of respectful wondering at it have caused me to lose some faith in the unquestioning atheism I inherited from my parents.

In his practice with patients, Dr. Farber was both far humbler than his more conventional colleagues and far bolder: He was humbler because he approached his patients as a whole human being, not as a semianonymous representative of his profession, and because he had abandoned his profession's claims to objectivity and curative power. He was bolder because when he took on a patient, he committed himself to a risky, open-ended friendship and to all the claims of responsibility that friendship entails. It was a brave venture to step from behind the mask of his profession, and a dangerous one.

Many other psychotherapists did something similar in the 1960s, of course, often with disastrous results. When professional barriers collapsed and there was no structure of personal rectitude to contain their passions and weaknesses, they often fell into misusing their patients—sleeping with them, or allowing themselves to be enthroned at the center of small worshipful cults by groups of patients who slept with one another, or, like Dr. S, allowing themselves to indulge in sentimental infatuations.

My impression has been that this kind of abuse was especially rife among the therapists of the existential school with which Farber was affiliated. He certainly shared their view that to understand people only in the reductive terms of the "medical model" is a drastic impoverishment of human possibility, but he never shared their woolly and inspirational leanings. He was tough-minded, and he held himself very carefully in check. His boundaries were moral, not professional. They were part of his being—not a stifling suit of armor but a flexible skin.

My sessions with Farber were utterly unlike my earlier experience of therapy. In the offices of my earlier therapists, I had understood that the world was to be kept at bay; pieces of it entered the room as carefully prepared specimens ready for examination and analysis. But in Dr. Farber's office, the world flowed in freely and surrounded us as we sat in those twin red leather chairs. Whatever scene he happened to be evoking—his favorite stretch of Broadway, a Riggs staff meeting, the shadowy contours of the domestic hallways that he negotiated late at night during his insomniac wanderings—would take shape in the space between us.

I had learned to think of my utterances as soap bubbles rotating in midair, to be examined by me with the help of the therapist. They were the matter of the enterprise. But with Dr. Farber, no such "work" was being undertaken. Instead, there was talk, and sometimes its freewheeling unpredictability disoriented me. The silences, which were more varied in tone than any I've ever known—some appreciative, some ruminative, some amused, some melancholy, some roiled by obscure tensions—were passages of open sea between the landmasses of talk. When I could see no horizon ahead, I was sometimes visited by moments of vertiginous panic.

We joked and gossiped and traded bits of trivia, but sometimes the tone of our talk deepened without warning. Once, in the middle of a session, in response to his secretary's soft tap on the door, Dr. Farber disappeared briefly and returned to his seat, his face ashen.

He told me he had just received news of his father's death. I got quickly to my feet and offered to leave, eager to show him I knew how to behave in this situation. He waved me back into my seat. "Stay," he said, and added, "please." We sat in silence for a good five minutes, and finally he began, haltingly, to talk about his father, about his family generally, and about death. I have very little memory of the specifics of what he said, only the residual feel of that half hour, the sympathy I felt, and also my distracting and shameful joy that he had done me the honor of confiding in me.

There was apparently no agenda in these sessions. My mind raced through possible sets of ordering rules, eliminating hypotheses as rapidly as it formed them. It seemed clear to me, for example, that any discussion of the interpersonal was off-limits, but then, quite out of the blue, Dr. Farber remarked that he found me to be a very guarded person (how this surprised and flattered me!) and that sometimes he wished I were more open.

Still, these talks were more than conversations. Dr. Farber listened with a heightened, if relaxed, alertness, and however widely we ranged over each hour's topics, he had a way of returning, almost musically, to the theme that united them.

Recently I've begun to figure out the connection between Dr. Farber's refusal to impose an agenda on the hour and his views on therapy, the will, and the imagination. His fundamental insight about human nature—that it is less susceptible, without distortion, to willed intervention than people in a therapeutic culture generally believe—shaped and limited what he could hope to accomplish through therapy. Much of what he did in the therapeutic hour resembled pastoral counseling; he guided and instructed. But he also exercised his imagination in extraordinary ways; whereas my other therapists had behaved as though there were no tense but the past, he was exquisitely on the uptake for clues about the future. I felt he was attending—with respect, and with a grave and humorous sympathy—the formation of my self.

Dr. Farber continued to toss books at me, and to ask me my opinions about them. He urged me to sign up for a music appreciation class at the local community college, and to take the exam for my GED certificate. I read the books, took the class, and passed the test, but these efforts were not enough to counteract the pull toward entropy that Riggs outpatient life exerted on me. I was spending far too much time hanging around the Inn, and although Dr. Farber deplored the passivity and emptiness of my existence, he admitted with a shrug that for me to live an active, engaged life as a Riggs patient would require a contortion of my will that he could not even begin to imagine.

Perhaps because he felt it would do me good, and get me out of the Inn, Dr. Farber offered me a kind of job. A famous theologian— I had heard of him and had the vaguest of impressions of his thinking—lived in Stockbridge. He was elderly now, bedridden after a stroke and very depressed. His wife had asked Dr. Farber if he would recommend a young person from Riggs who might visit with him for a few hours a week. She hoped it would do him some good to be reminded of his Union Theological Seminary students and the lively talks he used to have with them. She was also interested in finding a new boarder to live in their spare room, someone to do some light housework, run errands, and walk the dog.

When I arrived at the famous theologian's house, I was wearing a freshly washed and ironed navy blue skirt and white blouse, the most respectable outfit I owned. I had cleaned out my car, and as I approached the house, which was set off in a copse of pines a little distance from the town center, I took care to turn down my car radio.

The famous theologian's wife stood outside the door awaiting me. She was a charming Englishwoman in her fifties, full of bustle and good works, zealously attentive to her husband, intimidatingly well educated and widely read, inclined to quote Schopenhauer, to hum airs from Mozart, and to walk lightly on the balls of her feet. "Look hyah!" she called out as I approached. "She's terribly excited!" And I saw that a black standard poodle was slamming itself against the screen door, growling and slavering viciously. I froze for a moment. "Please don't mind her," said the famous theologian's wife, warmly offering me her hand. "She's just overwhelmed by youth and beauty. She sees so little of it."

I edged through the door as the famous theologian's wife held the dog. The smell of floor polish, the vista of shining floorboards, the thriving house plants, and the general air of cleanliness and order made me feel weak with longing for a moment, and the dog, baring its teeth and gums and straining so desperately against its collar that it gasped stertorously for breath, made me afraid. The famous theologian's wife (henceforth the FTW) seemed oblivious to the dog's blood-lust—I think she believed that a blithe and high-minded spiritual tolerance would always banish evil—but at one point the dog took a nip at my knee, and she was forced to remove it to the garage.

She ushered me into a darkened first-floor bedroom, where an old man rested in a shadowy bed. How do you do, I said softly, not knowing what else to say, and the occupant of the bed struggled to raise himself to a sitting position. "This is Miss Gordon," said the FTW, "who has been kind enough to drop by this afternoon."

Apparently that was all the exposure she thought appropriate for a first visit. She took me upstairs to look at the spare bedroom, which was airy and pleasant and very clean, with a view of the rose garden at the back of the property. The previous occupant had been a college student, the FTW told me, and a musician. A lovely person, but unfortunately a little careless about her living habits. She ate fruit in her room, and on more than one occasion had left the pits uncovered in the wastebasket.

I declined the room, using the excuse that my apartment lease held me to another six month's occupancy. But I did agree to show up the following Monday to spend fifteen minutes in the company of the FT. It seems impossible to me now that I had not taken the trouble to read even a page of any of his books in preparation for my visit, but this was the case. I remember thinking that if all else failed, we could talk about *I and Thou*, but the truth was that I had never gotten beyond page seventeen in that.

I sat down in the window seat, across the room from the bed where the theologian lay in silence. The FTW had placed a rocking chair at the side of the bed, but I was unable to bring myself to sit so intrusively close. For a time it seemed he was asleep, or dead, or at least unaware of my presence. I cleared my throat softly, and he turned in my direction, moving only his head. He gazed at me with a look that might have been interpreted as suspicion or mild hostility, or simply the befuddled wonderment of a man whose face could no longer register emotion readably; it was impossible to tell. I introduced myself, and he continued to stare.

Finally, he turned away. Time passed. I heard the doorbell ring, and the telephone. A delicious smell of baking crept under the door. The dog was released from the garage, and ran whining down the hall outside, her claws scrabbling on the hardwood floor. Outside, it was a clear, hot spring afternoon: A crew from the town seemed to be excavating a trench in the rose garden; I could imagine the smell of overturned earth, and I could hear wavering shouts and an occasional bark of laughter. The life of the household was pulsing around us, but in this room all was hush, as if the FT and I had found ourselves at the still point of the turning world.

Inwardly I rehearsed some possible opening gambits. "I'm a patient of Dr. Leslie Farber, and he . . . " Too roundabout, and also irrelevant. "I thought you might enjoy talking about . . . " About what? About all the theology I hadn't read? "Your wife tells me you once lived on Riverside Drive . . . " Pointless. Every possible entry to conversation seemed smug or stupid or offensive in one way or another. I began to conclude that he hated me, and quite understandably so—that my very presence in his room was presumptuous and an insult.

Afterward, when we were sitting at her kitchen table drinking cups of strong tea and eating the tiny ginger-flavored madeleines she had just taken from the oven, the FTW waved off my apologies. It was indeed a *very* difficult business, she said, adding that she had not failed to notice the delicacy I had shown in appreciating that. Perhaps it would be better to be a bit circumspect, to introduce me more gradually. She invited me to drink a glass of sherry with them on the following Sunday afternoon when he would be up and dressed and prepared to receive company.

That attempt, too, was a failure; in spite of the FTW's best efforts to promote the conversation, I proved once again to be as aphasic as the man sitting opposite me, propped in his wheelchair, upright now but eyeing me with the same suspicious wonderment I had seen in his face on my last visit.

The FTW put me on errand detail. My first job was to mail some letters and buy a dozen brass cuphooks. I found cuphooks, but they were not brass, and so I was sent to look farther afield, in Great Barrington and Pittsfield. I spent two days driving to perhaps seven hardware stores. I brought back a few packets of cuphooks that looked to me to be made of brass—the man behind the counter wasn't sure—but she rejected them. For the first time, she allowed herself to betray a little exasperation, not with me but with my country, where a cornucopia of vulgar consumer goods was forever spilling itself out, but where simple items important to the welfare of her household seemed not to be available.

Could I type, she asked. I answered that I could, a little, and she gave me packet of handwritten transcribed sermons to take home over the weekend. Almost immediately, I lost them in the chaos of my apartment. I failed to show up at the FT's the following Monday, or ever again, and for several months I hid from the FTW, instructing my roommates to tell her I was not at home when she called. My worst fear was that she might ask Dr. Farber what had become of me, but she never did. Perhaps her own sense of delicacy forbade that. One day when I was in the post office getting my mail, she confronted me, standing between me and the door so that no escape was possible. "Oh, Miss Gordon," she called out, smiling reassuringly and holding out a white-gloved hand. "We've been so anxious about you." I'm ashamed to say that I walked past her without even looking into her eyes. I drove back to my apartment and fell headlong onto my unmade bed, laughing and weeping, and shaking with guilt and rage.

I had told Dr. Farber every detail of my sexual misbehavior, but I never told him about how I let down the FT and the FTW. This was the first of two secrets I kept from him in the years I knew him, and this deception was a significant marker in my life: it was the first clear indication of a slowly widening split between the self that I presented in Dr. Farber's office and the self whose lack of competence in the world was to become increasingly problematic.

Around this time I once again joined my friends in their nightly visits to Simmy's, and once again I slept with some strangers I met there. But this second immersion in Stockbridge nightlife was different from the first, with less of what the Riggs authorities would have called "sexual acting-out" and more of an element of identification with the local scene.

My memories of those evenings are strangely gutted. I can remember how they began, with my arrival at Simmy's in the company of my roommates and assorted others. We ordered our beers from the grim-faced mustachioed Italian brother and sister who ran the place and sat in the grottolike back room, watching the band set up as the regulars filed in. I remember the next round as well, but the four hours after that are as vague as a smudged thumbprint, surely because I drank so much beer and because I was simultaneously so bored and so excited, standing in a line with my friends against the wall of the game room, watching the local bucks play pool and hoping to be noticed. My recollection resumes after closing time, but only in a fragmentary way; I remember waking as if from a dream at a woozy after-party in the local postmaster's darkened apartment, where in the middle of July all the doorways were strung with red and green Christmas lights.

From Dr. Farber, my anecdotes about Simmy's drew mixed reviews. Occasionally some detail intrigued him; he raised his eyebrows, or laughed, or paid me in kind with recollections about his younger days in the San Francisco bohemian group that revolved around the City Lights bookstore. (I got the better of that exchange.)

But mostly my Simmy's stories evoked fastidious grimaces and fatalistic sighs. Sometimes, if I pressed them too far, they triggered the "I'm not interested" reaction. But even when he recoiled from my accounts of drunken evenings at Simmy's, he was surprisingly tolerant; he sympathized with my boredom in Stockbridge, and more than any other middle-aged person I ever knew, he remembered, or was able to imagine, what it was like to be young.

I had the use of a white Ford Falcon station wagon, previously owned by my father, passed on to my sister, who kept it until she and her husband bought their own car, then—briefly—to my brother at Swarthmore, and then to me. This was the car in which my friends had driven me to New York for my appointment with the abortionist, and also the car in which Dr. S and I had tooled along over the leafy back roads of Lenox while I was learning to drive. I took my driving test in it too, Dr. S leaning anxiously forward in the back seat, talking me through gear changes and reminding me to keep right.

Dr. Farber rode in that car once too; after a therapy session one day, he asked me for a ride home. With a great sense of the honor of this occasion, I rushed out to the parking lot ahead of him and heaved a pile of detritus on the passenger seat into the back. Dr. Farber got in, politely ignoring the mess, and pulled the door shut. I turned the key in the ignition, and the radio, which I had forgotten to turn off, blasted top-twenty AM radio at earsplitting volume, causing me a moment of exquisite embarrassment.

My father passed the Falcon on to me with the proviso that I never drive it out of the state of Massachusetts without his permission, but I violated that injunction instantly and repeatedly. I treated it roughly, failed to keep up with the required maintenance and oil changes, and rode the clutch so incorrigibly that it had to be replaced twice. By the time I left Stockbridge to follow Dr. Farber to New York, it was an unsellable wreck. I have no memory of what happened to the Falcon; perhaps I gave it to some other patient, or simply abandoned it. It lives on as a piece of venerable space junk in the crowded universe of my memory, one of the earliest of my possessions to break loose from my erratic tracking system, soon to be joined by a multitude of other lost, spinning objects—the used cars I subsequently owned, the sprung couches, broken-spined books, scorched casseroles, and stained or shrunken items of clothing—all of which have passed out of my ownership and vanished.

A few months after my abortion, I drove the Falcon to the Albany airport to pick up my parents. Dr. Farber had summoned them for a meeting; they were flying in from different directions, my mother from Washington, and my father from some other city where he had been speaking. My mother had visited me in Stockbridge on a few occasions, to meet Dr. S and to help me get established in my first apartment, but my father had never yet been to see me at Riggs. This was the first time either of them had met Dr. Farber.

While I waited in front of the terminal building, I noticed that a long black limousine was parked ahead of me, all its doors flung open, and that four black men, glossily dressed in leather pants, pastel shirts, and gold chains, were ducking into it as the chauffeur loaded the trunk with luggage and musical instruments. It was Smokey Robinson and the Miracles! Unmistakably! I leaped from the Falcon and knocked on the tinted window of the limousine. Smokey Robinson himself opened it and smiled up at me. Those extraordinary hazel eyes, and small, perfect teeth! I introduced myself. "What's happenin', Emily?" he asked.

I was admitted into the limousine and invited to sit on the jump seat. When I had calmed down enough to get control of my voice, I told the Miracles that I had watched them perform at the Howard Theater in Washington more Saturday afternoons than I could count. I got their autographs on a grocery receipt, the only piece of paper I could find in my purse. "Love Ya," Smokey wrote, and appended his swirling signature.

Would I like to come along with them to Utica, where they had a gig that night? If I had not looked up at that moment to see my father's face peering angrily into the window of the limousine, I might well have accepted the invitation, leaving my parents stranded and the unlocked Falcon blocking a line of traffic, with its engine running and my purse gaping open on the front seat.

Dr. Farber met with my parents and me in the conference room on the first floor of the Riggs medical building. We all sat at one end of the same enormous table where I had faced the assembled Riggs staff at my first-year conference. My mother looked tense and composed; she wore her Peck & Peck herringbone tweed suit and carried a dark straw bag. I wore my mushroom-scented jeans. My father looked impatient and distracted; he had brought his bulging attaché case to the meeting, and while we waited for Dr. Farber to arrive, he pulled out a thick document, put on his half-glasses, and began to read, underlining passages in pen.

My parents had spent the night at a local motel, and they had arrived at my apartment a few hours before the meeting to take me out to breakfast. I had made some efforts to clean the apartment, but when my father reached the top of the stairs and craned his neck to get a look at the kitchen, with its loaded, jumbled surfaces and furry floor, he winced. So, he said. This is how you live.

Dr. Farber arrived. He and my parents exchanged introductory pleasantries, some talk of Washington, D.C.—my parents, it turned out, went to the same dentist Dr. Farber had used, and frequented the same discount liquor store. Dr. Farber then went on to explain to my parents why he had arranged this meeting. He began by remarking that I was a young person with some marked aptitudes—aptitudes that were as undeveloped as they were striking, he added. Both my parents nodded.

He was concerned that I seemed to have no picture of the future; he had the impression I had never imagined my life after the age of thirty. Dr. Farber turned inquiringly to me, and after a moment's thought, I nodded. (The truth was—though it was too laughably melodramatic a notion to express—that thirty seemed an infinitely remote age to me, and I assumed I would be dead before I reached it.)

He turned to my father: What do you think Emily will do with her life? How do you envision her future? My father looked nonplussed, and a little panicky. When he answered, his tone was uncharacteristically wary and hesitant. Whatever Emily hopes to do, he said, she will have to learn to organize herself and budget her money, and she will have to make a plan to get through at least two years of college.

I think perhaps you misunderstood my question, said Dr. Farber. Let me repeat it: What do you think Emily will do with her life?

Perhaps something literary, my mother interjected, but Dr. Farber ignored her, and continued to look steadily at my father. My father stiffened slightly. I don't think it makes sense, he said, to talk about what Emily is going to do until Emily prepares herself to do something.

The standoff went silent for a while. For a few awkward moments all of us kept ourselves occupied with our cigarettes—how can such ordeals be gotten through, as they are today, without the distraction and comfort of smoking? I saw that my father was going progressively redder in the face.

When Dr. Farber and I talked about the meeting later, we found that past this point both of our recollections began to grow gaps. Even between us, we could not fully reconstruct the course of the discussion. We certainly both remembered my father's explosion, his shouted assertion that I had come out of my mother's womb hating him, but we had forgotten exactly what led up to it, and what immediately followed. We also both recalled another high point of the interview, when my father compared himself—and it seems hard to believe that he could make so quick a transition from rage to the after-dinner-speech expansiveness of this extended analogy—to an airport control tower and his children to airplanes. Emily, he said, is a little airplane that got out of range of the tower. We also both remembered Dr. Farber's interjection here: And what is Mrs. Gordon, he asked, the hangar?

At the end of the interview, when we were all walking out of the door of the conference room, we heard the approaching siren of the fire truck from the direction of Main Street. This was a familiar sound in Stockbridge; the volunteer firemen's association was a proud pillar of local civic life, and the truck seemed to barrel down Main Street at least twice a week, whether a fire was actually in progress or not. The siren galvanized my father. He rushed to the window to watch the truck go by. I love a fire! he said. I love to follow the truck and watch the fire! Suppressing a dangerous half-smile, Dr. Farber sidled over to me and murmured into my ear. That explains a lot, he said. My father overheard that remark, and he muttered angrily about it for the remainder of the visit.

*   *   *

Dr. Farber began the session after the meeting with my parents by musing aloud about another patient whose parents had recently visited. This was a young man whom both Dr. Farber and I knew to be gay and in the process of acknowledging his homosexuality to himself. During the session, he had mustered the courage to tell his parents. What impressed Dr. Farber was the father's reaction. This man, the owner of a construction company and a person with little formal education, absorbed his son's news and said, "Well, whatever Jonathan is, I love him."

Dr. Farber told me that story, and we both sat in silence for a while, wiping our eyes. This was one of those ur-tales—Dr. Farber would have called it "constitutive"—that I carried away from my association with Dr. Farber. It gave me a vision of family love that was just as new to me and just as ineradicable as the vision of madness that he had conveyed when we talked about Pat.

And of course the light it threw on my parents was not flattering. After that Riggs visit—I believe it was the spring after my nineteenth birthday—I began the process of giving up on my parents. I had already begun to reach the conclusion that too little fabric remained—this was the metaphor that always came to my mind—for my relation to my parents ever to be repaired.

Dr. Farber seemed to concur. He had summoned my parents to this meeting to give them a last chance to redeem themselves in his eyes, to satisfy himself that I had portrayed them accurately. I saw my parents in a new way, as if I were looking at them simultaneously through Dr. Farber's eyes and my own. My father appeared as a bright and decent man with a boobish lack of interiority. My mother seemed not only unhappy but also selfish and willfully self-destructive, her fey charm calculated and manipulative. My parents' marriage—mystery that it still remains to me—

had turned out to be destructive to both parties, a kind of reverse synergy, where both fed and both starved. I understood Dr. Farber's story about Jonathan as carrying a homiletic double message; perhaps if I could separate myself from my parents, I might eventually find the future I had been incapable of imagining, and perhaps it might bring me a chance at another kind of family.

Dr. Farber was an inspired complainer. His grumblings about Stockbridge had been a staple of our talks from the beginning, but as the months went by his disaffection became comically obsessive. He began to swear that he would be gone by the time the leaves changed in the fall, that he refused to endure another round of rhapsodizing about the foliage.

It was not that the town was sleepy, he insisted. He had come here, after all, to escape some of the distractions that had been sapping his writing energies in Washington. What bothered him was that Stockbridge was such a Potemkin village. There were no jobs here, no industry, unless you counted tourism and mental illness. Everyone seemed to be rich and idle. Or at least idle, he amended; he had encountered a few toothless rustics lounging outside Nejaimes, the general store—placed there by the Chamber of Commerce, no doubt. He had grown sick of Norman Rockwell, sick of maple sugar and ski talk and the carloads of leaf-peepers who clogged Main Street in the fall. Sick of not being able to find a decent corned beef sandwich.

So it should have come as no surprise to me when Dr. Farber announced that he was moving to New York City, where he would set up a private practice and continue his writing, but for some reason it did. I can't remember whether he invited me to follow, or whether I invited myself, or whether I simply assumed that I would come along, but I did. And so, in fact, did both of his other Riggs patients.

What would I do in New York? I would find a job, of course. Where would I live? I would find an apartment.

Now that my daughter is close to the age I was when I went to Riggs, I find myself wondering whether I wouldn't have been better off being introduced to independence by degrees—living as an au pair, for example, with a warm, stable family. This seems reasonable to the woman I have become (better than reasonable, in fact; I covet it retrospectively). But to the girl I was, it would have been intolerable. In middle age it's easy to forget how wild I was, how chaotic, how full of violent excitements. And Dr. Farber was not the man to arrange such a situation for me. He was wry and delicate and quiet, but in his own way he was also a swashbuckler. He was a liberator, not a social worker. He never adapted his treatment style to accommodate my age and immaturity. Instead, he looked a little beyond the person I was and addressed the person I would become.

After my last session with Dr. Farber in Stockbridge, I invited him to a small farewell party my roommates and I had arranged. We had spent a week cleaning the apartment; one of us baked a cake, which had collapsed in the center and been repaired with a heavy application of frosting. We also bought a bottle of champagne, a semiexpensive jar of caviar, and, as an afterthought, a box of tea bags in assorted flavors, in case he preferred to drink something nonalcoholic.

What a child I still was! It never occurred to me that Dr. Farber might have another appointment immediately after my hour, or some other commitment, or that he simply might not accept my invitation. But as it happened he did; we walked slowly down Main Street toward my apartment, and I remember feeling an extraordinary sense of peace and happiness in Dr. Farber's company that afternoon. It seemed to me that my friendship with him had proven itself to be portable, and that a future was materializing ahead of me into which I could carry it. This short, silent, companionable walk with a serious friend—the most trustworthy one I had ever found, and the only teacher from whom I had ever been able to accept instruction—was a moment worth preserving in memory.

6

NEW YORK

When I arrived in the city I took a cab from Port Authority to the Paris Hotel on the Upper West Side—somebody had recommended it as cheap and international in its clientele. My room was an airshaft special, so narrow that I had to edge around the bed sideways. I shared a bathroom at the end of the hall with a group of big rough German girls. Luckily for me, they rarely bathed.

I crossed Broadway in the mornings, bought a cardboard container of coffee and a cheese Danish at a coffee shop and picked up the *New York Times*, returned to my room, and spent the morning smoking Marlboros—I can see the jaunty red and white carton now, on the window sill over the hissing, clanking radiator—and searching the classifieds. I made a list of the likeliest prospects and took it down to the lobby, where I joined the line waiting to use the pay phone. I came to recognize the elderly men who frequented the lobby of the Paris—shrunken, toothpick-chewing characters in suede caps who claimed the sprung armchairs early in the morning and spent the day perusing the racing form and bantering with the doorman.

I found that I was not the only recently released mental patient walking the streets of New York. It was the fall of 1968: The psychiatric wards had recently been emptied by deinstitutionalization, the patients released into what psychiatrists called "the community." The benches of the pocket parks along Broadway were lined with lunatics—mutterers, twitchers, hallucinators, impassioned monologuists, silent dazed sufferers. I remember encountering the first bag lady I had ever seen. I stared wonderingly at her swollen ankles, flecked with open sores, her layers of charcoal-gray garments, and what I could see of her face, mysteriously lowered and only half visible in the shadows of the cave formed by the blankets she had wrapped around her head.

She was so unprecedented a sight that at first I took her to be a member of some obscure religious sect. (I made other such mistaken speculations early in my New York days—wondering, for example, why so many Amish men seemed to be employed in the garment district.) But soon enough I realized she was simply a penniless madwoman, a Pat without a trust fund, and that what had happened to her body and clothes was a consequence of living in the cold wind and blowing grit of Broadway without shelter or self-maintenance. Years later, when I had seen many of her more seasoned sisters, I realized that this woman had been a pioneer shopping-bag lady, still relatively young and new to the life. Her skin was gray but not yet blackened by the elements, and her legs, though puffy and wounded, had not yet stiffened into edematous columns.

One night when loneliness and sleeplessness had driven me out of my room at the Paris to the coffee shop, and I was sitting at the counter eating a piece of lemon meringue pie, this woman wandered in from the cold street and stood out of the way of traffic behind the coatrack. The proprietor caught sight of her—she was doing her best to be inconspicuous, but I could smell her ten feet away—and barked at her to leave. "Outa here! Get out!" he shouted, making sweeping gestures with his arms. The woman stood her ground, feigning deafness perhaps, staring stolidly down at her split canvas shoes. The proprietor kept after her like a dog yapping at the heels of an addled cow: Clearly this happened often, and her part in the game was to resist his hectoring long enough to get warm.

I was in a mood to feel sympathetic toward the bag lady that evening: I had spent the day waiting in the hallway outside a temporary-employment agency to be sent on job interviews and the evening lying on my unmade bed at the Paris, smoking obsessively and considering a plan to take what remained of my money and spend it on a bus ticket back to Stockbridge. I watched her as she shuffled out again into the night, my eyes filling with indignant tears. Impulsively, I ordered a hamburger and french fries to go and walked down Broadway in search of her, carrying the food in a rapidly cooling brown paper bag. She was gone from her usual bench. I walked a few blocks until I saw her familiar hulking silhouette through the window of another coffee shop. I hesitated; it seemed somehow quixotic to offer the food to her now that she had moved on to another warm lighted place, and even more pointless to wait outside. What had begun as a mission of impulsive kindness now seemed like a clumsy intrusion—she had her routine, I realized, and my well-meaning gesture could only cramp her style. I returned to my room at the Paris, and even though by now the food was not only cold but chilled, and utterly unappetizing, I ate the hamburger and french fries. I found, as I turned off the light and tried once more to sleep, that a decision had formed in my mind; I would hold onto my money and stay in New York.

I was lonely, anxious, and disoriented in those early New York days, but also braced and exhilarated. I felt dilated, open to the smells and atmospheres and street vistas of New York in a new way, as if a layer of batting had been removed from my senses. My new solitude and the stringencies of my life in the city had intensified my identification with myself. The inner commentator that had begun to speak in my childhood and that had been silent for so many years was beginning to be audible again, but now that voice was not only a companion but also a warning, scolding, comforting adviser. I talked myself through subway changes and job interviews and insomniac hours in my bed at the Paris.

During my first months in New York, I found I was reluctant to reestablish my therapy with Dr. Farber—I wanted to find a job and an apartment first. Then I would be able to realize the fantasy that mobilized me in my most discouraged moments: I would sit opposite Dr. Farber in his new office, in one of the familiar leather chairs, and I would proudly display for him my newly independent life.

I became a hypervigilant creature of coffee and cigarettes. My attachment to alcohol was severed by New York; now it had become associated in my mind with the corner bars on Broadway, grim little caves lit by neon shamrocks and populated at night by the same phlegmy old men who spent their mornings in the lobby of the Paris. Once I had made the decision to stay in New York, I began to look back on my easy Stockbridge existence as shamefully indolent and purposeless. It seemed so distant that I felt I must have forsaken it not weeks but years ago.

I had never felt the grain and texture of things so distinctly, never lived a life in which the stakes seemed so nearly real—I say "nearly" because in the back of my mind I always knew that if things got very bad, I could call my father, and that after a fifteen-minute ordeal of harsh sighs and suspicious questions about my efforts to find a job, he would agree to send a check to cover my expenses for the next two weeks.

I looked for work conscientiously, but I had no skills, no college degree, not even a legitimate high school diploma, only the GED certificate Dr. Farber had kept after me to acquire. I followed up on likely-looking ads in the *Times* classified section: "well-spoken, dynamic admin. asst. for creative ad agency," and "good English skills a must for aide to editor in publ. co." I waited in midtown office buildings to be called into interviews, where I was sized up and rejected in the same instant. That was no wonder; I was a rumpled mess with a chronic cough, a self-inflicted pixie haircut, and a three-year gap in my history that I refused, on principle, to lie about or even to explain in the space provided on the application form.

My first job, when I finally found it, was not one that required an immaculate wardrobe or an advanced degree. "Lab tech. with no exp." read the ad in the *New York Times*. I recognized myself in that description, and I was hired on the spot, in a converted loft laboratory above Canal Street, where I put on a dingy white coat and ran experiments on transmission-oil samples. That job paid sixty-eight dollars a week, take-home. My co-workers were newly arrived immigrants, most with no English. When the first snow fell in late November, they all left their stations and stood in a row in the diffuse white light of the great loft windows, watching as the flakes came slanting down. They were Ghanaian, Jamaican, Filipino, Thai; none of them had ever seen snow before.

Most days I manned the "viscosometer," a machine that measured the relative viscosity of three different kinds of oil at the same time. Stopwatch in hand, I poured the samples into small heated metal wells, timed the oil as it ran down three tilted metal grooves, then recorded my findings in a notebook. I became so oil-saturated that my face broke out, and my hands were too greasy to grip the metal pole on the subway.

I found that job several months after I left the Paris. In the meantime, I moved from one stopgap living situation to another. The Farbers, who had sublet a brownstone on 94th Street between Columbus and Amsterdam, hired me to stay with their three young children (Dr. Farber's wife—his second—was considerably younger than he) while they went to Paris for a week. They overpaid me so lavishly that I was able to support myself for another month.

They also brokered a deal between me and Dr. Farber's brother Manny, an artist and movie critic. In exchange for free lodging in the Soho studio where he was showing his paintings, I agreed to act as hostess for the exhibition. I slept on a mattress in the center of the empty, echoing loft, woke early in the mornings and dragged the mattress into the back room where the artist stored his supplies, and did my best to wash in the deep sink where he rinsed out his brushes. I put on a dress and panty hose and a pair of black pumps, peered into a fragment of broken, cloudy mirror to apply my lipstick, and stationed myself in a chair by the door, where I remained from ten until six, admitting a trickle of visitors to the show and passing out brochures. As "hostess" I did my best to make myself invisible. I knew nothing about painting, and I was terribly afraid someone might assume that I could answer questions.

By the time the exhibition ended, I still knew nothing about Manny Farber's paintings, but I had come to know them in the way a dairy farmer knows each member of his herd. They were large ovals executed on brown paper—speckled, pitted fields of muted, variegated color (rather like my early egg, it occurs to me now). They were austere and evocative, the product of a powerfully unified vision, but each one was absolutely distinct and charged with its own atmosphere, like a first view of the rough surface of a newly discovered planet.

The loft itself was a space so big and high and empty that I felt theatrically self-conscious walking from one end of it to the other. Once I yielded to an impulse to dance an orbit around the splintery parquet floor in my bare feet, pausing in front of each painting to execute a deep bow and arm sweep.

Sometimes in the middle of a long quiet afternoon, trapped in the studio with no phone and no distractions, a fugue of impression would begin to build. Manny Farber's paintings, the space around me, the smell of my own sweat, the itch of dust in my throat, the rumble of traffic and the brief cacophonous bursts of car horns below me in the street, the cropped view of leafless trees and red brick and chilly sky that the light-blocking shades on the windows of the loft permitted me—all these elements swarmed and buzzed and swelled into epiphany. The city itself came to visit me in the empty loft, bringing with it a vague and transporting sense of the future.

At night, released from my captivity, I went out and found myself a sandwich or a cheap Chinese meal. The neighborhood was given over to small retail outlets, where myriad, mystifying hardware items were displayed in plastic buckets and sold for a quarter apiece. I picked up these objects and examined them, wondering what this macaroni-shaped piece of pipe was intended for, or this thing like a tuning fork, or these little plastic slugs. The world, the world! These objects were instruments of its purposes, so many of which I would never know.

Another person in my circumstance might have tried to make

herself comfortable in the loft—bought a radio, a supply of snacks and magazines. This never occurred to me. In the back of my mind I think I believed that any attempt to control or alter experience would distort it, and obscure the lesson it held in store for me.

I moved into my first New York apartment, a tiny two-room place on the top floor of an East Village walk-up with a loft bed built into a closet. The toilet was out in the hall in a sky-blue cubicle somebody had decorated with careful copies of the graphics from "Yellow Submarine." My roommate and I shared it with the elderly Ukrainian woman who lived down the hall amid icons and cabbage fumes, and a transvestite junkie who used it to shoot up in.

My roommate was Susan, a Stockbridge native. I had met her once or twice at Simmy's during my Riggs years, and when I ran into her on the steps of the New York Public Library and told her about my efforts to find a job and an apartment, she generously invited me to sleep on her couch. I stayed for a year, and paid my half of the forty-dollar monthly rent.

Susan was gentle and dignified and sometimes a little absent. She had moved to the East Village with a much older man, the owner of an arty bookstore who plunged into all the practices of the hip life and expected Susan to do the same. She was too faithful and old-fashioned and genuinely in love with this man to comply, and so he left her, and she joined the legions of young women injured by the sexual revolution.

Susan's tangled blonde hair fell below her waist; she wore long India-print skirts and quilted vests and intricate dangling earrings and contact lenses that she was forever losing. She worked at a secondhand fur store in the West Village when I first met her;

later she quit that job and did freelance editing and indexing. As a slob, she ran a close second to me, but she had a flair for detail, and she was not without domestic talents. Her apartment had curtains on its windows and built-in bookshelves and a well-equipped kitchen, but it was so small and so full of her packrat collections of magazines and piles of papers waiting to be sorted and the malodorous old mouton coats she had bought at a discount that its organizational infrastructure was on the point of being overwhelmed. When I moved in, bringing my own more freewheeling style of slovenliness, the balance was tipped.

One of Susan's bosses was an editor named Roz, a woman only a few years older than we were but so forthrightly careerist and prematurely sensible in her business suits and alligator pumps that we viewed her as a member of another generation. She sometimes dropped off manuscripts at the apartment, staying politely to drink a cup of coffee with us. (Susan observed the small-town custom of inviting anyone who knocked at the door to come in and sit down. More than once I came home to find her pouring herbal tea for our transvestite junkie neighbor.) I could not help noticing Roz's efforts to conceal her queasy alarm as she sat at the table—the only uncluttered surface in the apartment—casting uneasy glances at the kitchen bathtub and the box turtle that Susan kept in it, while Susan stepped delicately around the cat's overflowing litter box and crusted food dishes, waiting on her guest as placidly as any farm wife with pies cooling on her windowsill.

I think of Roz now because I've come, in later years, to be surrounded by academic overachievers, many of whom apparently slogged through the 1960s with their heads down, following the track of some ambition so doggedly that all the craziness of that time passed over them and left them unchanged. These people have tended to gravitate toward mathematics and the sciences and the analytic wing of philosophy. (The former revolutionaries, I've noticed, seem to end up as administrators.)

My own attitude toward the 1960s was ambivalent at first, and gradually become more and more contrarian. I identified with the anarchic energies of the period—the music, the colors, the strobe lights, the hair, and the dancing. I began by finding a certain comfort in being part of a generation that had disowned its parents; surrounded by the youth culture, I could blur the painful reality that it was actually my parents who had disowned me. But soon enough, of course, something in my viscera executed a flip, and I found myself outside the world of my generation, looking in with a familiar disenfranchised longing, and also a certain resentment.

Even at Riggs I had resisted the idea of taking therapeutic drugs. I certainly did my share of drinking, but I was the only patient I knew who went without medication throughout my entire hospitalization. (It occurs to me now that my native aversion to drugs was surely one of the reasons Dr. Farber chose me as a patient. He took a very hard line on the use of tranquilizers and sedatives.) Living in the East Village, I found that I also felt obscurely disinclined to take the recreational drugs on offer there. The few times I smoked marijuana I was terrified by my inability to keep track of the syntax of my sentences.

I began to feel that the whole notion of psychedelic enlightenment had something totalitarian at its heart, that under the influence of drugs I would be expected to discover no difference between my subjectivity and everyone else's. Marijuana was a powerful leveler: Having smoked it, everybody's head was assumed to be populated by throbbing neon mandalas and ranks of dancing cartoon mice; according to its etiquette, everybody was expected to smile beatifically and say, "Wow!" My instinct was to protect my consciousness from colonization by Zapp Comix imagery. I sensed that a life of drug ingestion would knock down the partitions in my brain and flood it with light, that I would no longer be able to visit the shadowy rooms of reverie at the back of my mind.

But even if I had wanted to join the youth culture, I had come to the East Village a little too late to find it. A year after its passing, it was hard to understand what the "summer of love" could have meant. The place was just too scary and crime-ridden and filthy, and it seemed to me that it would take a powerful hallucinogen indeed to make Avenue C, where squadrons of Hell's Angels massed on the corners, revving their bikes and throwing back quart bottles of ale, feel like a haven of peace and love. I had arrived just as the movement was shifting its focus from urban collective to rural commune. The hippies were decamping for Vermont, to try their hands at organic farming. They took their enchantments with them, returning the streets of the East Village to their aboriginal bleakness.

Eventually I was to find the political aspect of the youth movement even more off-putting than the ecstatic, druggy wing. Later in my New York years, after I had moved out of the East Village and into an apartment far uptown near Fort Tryon Park and the Cloisters, I found a job at Columbia University in the Academic Placement Office, where I photocopied and collated the dossiers of graduate students who were applying for teaching jobs. I also filed, and fetched coffee from Chock full o' Nuts. I was the lowest-ranking person in the office, but this was the most respectable job I had yet found, and the best-paying.

I was always on the point of losing it because of my chronic lateness, and I was in particular jeopardy just when one of the student uprisings began. A new director had recently been installed, a middle-aged woman with a background in business administration and a mandate to tidy up the routines and appearances of the office. She fired off memos ordering changes in our dress and deportment—no more open-toed shoes or bare legs, no more eating meatball subs at our desks, no more inappropriate levity in the halls. She put us all on notice that even if the students succeeded in closing down the university, we were expected to come to work, and she took me aside to let me know that one more episode of lateness would be my last.

And so began my brief career as a scab. The first morning of the shutdown, I stood outside Dodge Hall, blocked from the entrance by a moat of shouting protesters that stretched all the way around the building. "Shut it down!" they shouted, swaying in their comradely ranks as I waited timidly for the right moment to make a run for it; sometimes I succeeded, ducking and dodging through the line, but more often I failed. Once I was elevated in a chair of interlocked hands and given the heave-ho, landing with an arm-flailing stagger several feet away on the icy grass. After that, there was nothing to do but try again. When I finally reported for work, I found that only my boss was present; apparently she had driven in from New Jersey before dawn.

The image of the rosy, angry young faces of those protesters has remained in my mind ever since, and I can still feel the stinging freshness of my resentment. Like them, I opposed the Vietnam War, but the notion of closing down the university to end it struck me as patently ridiculous—like masturbating to end the population explosion, as somebody later put it.

What gave me particular pain was that I could not help recognizing the personal sources of my political resentments. These protesters, wrapped up warmly in mufflers and tasseled hats, were all so obviously affluent and well-cared for. If their beards were scruffy, their teeth were white and orthodontically straightened. (My gums bled every time I brushed my teeth.) The strength of this resentment has made me uncertain of my politics ever since; I can never be sure that my views are based in anything but reaction.

I knew these young men, and what I felt toward them was something like blue-collar scorn. They were the high achievers who could be always depended on to scribble a few sentences after the exam proctor called time. Their brief careers as insurrectionists would have no lasting effect on their lives; in twenty-five years they would sit in boardrooms and corner offices, looking back on their days of rage with fond detachment. Revolutionaries, indeed! They were loved children, every one. Watching them, I first felt that rancorous self-pity that has been the emotional legacy of the 1960s.

Under my simple envious anger, I was also beginning to sense the depth of my estrangement from the politics of the youth culture. I was coming to hate the bullying notion that one was either part of the problem or part of the solution, that one was to lead, follow, or get out of the way, that to be apolitical was itself a political position. I was beginning to know myself now, to recognize that I was the kind of person who accepted what Dr. Farber would have called "the given." My ambition was not to change the world but to describe it.

Dr. Farber and I were spending a lot of time on the subject of demonstrations, drugs, and the youth culture generally. Since the move to New York, his view of the 1960s had shifted from bemused curiosity to something closer to scorn. Was I merely reflecting his influence? Not in this case, I believe—though I certainly tended to imitate him, and to parrot his favorite phrases. I brought my own set of preoccupations to my attitudes about my cohort in the 1960s, and something quite genuinely and independently curmudgeonly in me was roused into being by the splashy, self-indulgent, and conformist dissent I saw all around me. Part of what had drawn me to Dr. Farber in the first place was a half-conscious recognition of a fellow scoffer, one with the authority to liberate and make legitimate the contrarian in me.

Soon after I moved into Susan's apartment, she left for the weekend, and my old Stockbridge friend Caroline came to visit. We had just returned from dinner at Katz's Delicatessen and a walk around the neighborhood. I was briefly enjoying the novel sensation of having the upper hand in our friendship: Caroline had been impressed by the corned beef sandwich and Dr. Brown's Cel-Ray tonic I ordered for her at Katz's and gratifyingly appalled by the junkies nodding on the stoop. She hung back as we stepped around them on our way into the building. They were absolutely harmless, I reassured her, too stoned to move. Caroline was on my own newly won territory now; I got to demonstrate my urban savvy while she was left with the role of the wide-eyed country cousin.

Just as we were taking off our coats, we heard a knock at the door. I opened it, and two men shouldered their way into the apartment, one of whom, I realized, was the more alert-looking of the junkies we had passed a few moments earlier. He was pointing a gun with a long silencer at us, and his companion had a knife. They shoved us onto the couch. Don't move, they warned us. Don't move and— they actually used this phrase—nobody gets hurt.

I was too terrified not to giggle. Caroline was indignant. How *dare* they, she stage-whispered as the two men rifled through my roommate's bureau drawer and systematically overturned kitchen canisters. I dug my fingernails into the back of her hand and hissed at her to shut up. I hated her for her reflexive sense of entitlement, which I was sure would presently get us killed. Looking down at her hand, I realized, with a sinking heart, that she was wearing two expensive rings and a gold bracelet.

Before I could signal to her to take them off, to hide them, the man with the gun returned, holding the shoe box in which my roommate kept her bound quarters and fifty-cent pieces. How much in here, he asked. Oh, fifty dollars, at least, I said, estimating blithely, though I had no idea. Anything else? I pointed at my purse, which the gunman stooped to pick up, still keeping his eyes fixed on us. He fished out my wallet.

How about yours? Caroline hesitated, and then pulled her purse from behind the sofa cushion. The sight of the gun had persuaded her. Apparently satisfied with our wallets and Susan's box of coins, the two men backed out of the apartment, but not before the one who had been doing the talking offered an apology, an explanation, and a warning. We know you're good people, he said. Understand. We're doing this for a brother in jail.

While his partner waited by the door, his face sullen and unreadable, the spokesman came back into the room and handed me a joint of marijuana, smiling sweetly when I accepted it. The sight of his small picket teeth made me realize I had seen him several times before, coming out of the apartment of the transvestite junkie.

Finally they left; the door closed behind them, but just as Caroline and I were rising to our feet, it opened again. The spokesman leaned into the room and waggled the gun at us. Don't call the police, he said. We'll know and we'll come back and kill you.

We waited ten minutes before we called. When the police did come, some twenty minutes later, they shook their heads regretfully at our delay in calling. Those guys are long gone, they said. No point in going after them now. One of them caught sight of

Caroline's hand. Hey, he said, raising his eyebrows skeptically, I see you've still got your jewelry.

The robbery marked the beginning of my dependent collapse onto the Farbers. It was also the beginning of an intensely rewarding friendship with Dr. Farber's wife Anne, which I still enjoy today. She was the one who received Caroline and me when we appeared at her door that night, embraced and comforted us, gave us each a restorative snifter of brandy, and sat with us while we told our conflicting accounts of the event. It was then that I first appreciated how intensely she listens, with a grand theatricality—she leaned into our narratives, gripping our hands and wincing at our terror—and a passionately genuine concern. This was the first of many talks with Anne, and I came to appreciate not only her generosity but also the clarity and rigor of her intellect and the delicacy of her tact.

Anne was in her late thirties then, less than twenty years my senior, a beautiful, vivid woman of Manx ancestry, thriving in her marriage and harried motherhood, a musician and accompanist and all-purpose intellectual. She was in the habit of reading several books simultaneously, keeping them at various stations around the apartment—one in the bedroom, one in the living room, one in the kitchen. Her energy was staggering; she was like a many-armed Indian goddess, one hand stirring a sauce, one composing a sentence, several holding open books, another feeling a feverish child's forehead. She was a collection of broken or transcended expectations, managing to be simultaneously self-dramatizing and sincere, a woman of action and a true contemplative. Gradually, I began to understand the importance of her contribution to Dr. Farber's writing and thinking. Their marriage was absolutely traditional in one sense—I never saw Dr. Farber so much as rinse out a saucer—but intellectually it was strikingly egalitarian. It would not be accurate to say the Farbers were collaborators, but it was true that his work grew out of dialogue with her.

After the robbery I began to spend more time at the Farbers'. I was very fond of the three Farber children, and always happy to sit for them, but soon enough, I began to feel I needed no excuse to drop by. The Farbers had moved by now to a ten-room, high-ceilinged Upper West Side apartment in a building between Broadway and West End, an easy place to find oneself late in the afternoon, not only for me but for many interesting people. I was reassured to notice that other patients felt free to visit, perhaps not quite as frequently as I did, but often enough. Various intellectuals, writers, artists, musical people, and Jesuit priests—Dr. Farber seemed to like to keep a few of these around—also began to appear.

The Farbers' living room became an informal salon, a setting for contentious debate and intimate, self-revealing talk. These discussions were a revelation to me; I had never realized that it was possible for a group of smart, witty, intellectually combative people to join in a project of talking their way toward the truth. Now I understood how starved I had been for talk: The discussion at my parents' table had been severely circumscribed. As for my own generation, they were doing their best to stay below the level of the verbal. Their talk was gestural, full of sloganeering and self-justification; they celebrated their inarticulateness and made a stiff, blundering golem out of moral discrimination.

I was too shy to contribute much, but I sat and listened. On a few occasions I gathered the courage to blurt something out, and once, with Dr. Farber's encouragement—he actually held up a hand and silenced the cross talk in order to give me a chance to break out of my hemming and hawing—I said something valuable. I've long since forgotten what it was, but I still remember the intoxicating sensation of watching as several pairs of thoughtfully widened eyes turned toward me.

I was "shy"? I "listened"? I can't let these inaccuracies pass uncorrected. I was never shy; what looked like shyness was intense self-consciousness and self-doubt and—struggling against these constraints—a ferocious ambition to be heard. I listened only intermittently (perhaps this is why I learned so little), pouncing on remarks and pawing them over for what was of use in them to me. By the time I had torn open a particular unit of discourse, swallowed the nutrient, and discarded the residue, the conversation had moved on and I had missed some essential connective.

Anne, with her generous energies, took the lead in these evenings. Dr. Farber rarely stayed until the end. He had an odd way of rising abruptly from his seat, bowing to the assembled company, and simply walking out of the room. It seemed to me sometimes as I watched him (and my eyes were always returning to his face) that he was suddenly overwhelmed with weariness and something close to disgust, that he had been registering not only the content of the discussion but also the sparring of egos, and that he suddenly had endured all of that he could bear. (Not that he was egoless himself; he had a weakness, in fact, for the company of celebrities, and his one besetting minor sin was name-dropping.) Perhaps it was not only the competitiveness of the enterprise that drove him away; it seemed to me sometimes that he found the energy of these discussions—an energy fueled by alcohol, in the case of some of the participants—a little crude and overwhelming. I think he withdrew to protect the privacy of his most closely held beliefs.

Often I was one of the last people present at the end of the evening. I helped Anne clean up—it was amazing what a mess a group of people arriving in staggered ranks over the course of the evening, some for drinks and some for dinner and some for after-dinner coffee and brandy, could generate. In return for this service, I got to participate in the postmortem, always my favorite part of any evening. Anne solicited my opinions about the guests: What is your impression of M, she would ask, for example. (M was a famous psychoanalyst, handsome, charismatic, and self-infatuated, with white hair sprawling over his collar. He had recently married a much younger and very pneumatic blonde.) I reflected for a moment and said I had nothing of interest to say about B, but I'd noticed that his wife looked like something off a pinball machine. I knew I would get a laugh for this, and I did.

And sometimes after the dishwasher had been loaded and the surfaces scrubbed, I stayed on until very late, talking with Anne. These were long, deep, confessional conversations. She told me the story of her romance with Leslie Farber: Some ten years earlier, as his patient, she had fallen in love with him. He terminated the therapy after three months without explanation, she told me, and when, six years later, they found one another again, he confessed he had been in love with her as well—all this time—and that it was for this reason he had fired her as his patient.

Though I did my best to conceal it, my reaction to this story was mild shock and a faint queasiness. While I recognized and responded to his masculine elegance, I was so backward as never to have contemplated the idea of Dr. Farber as an erotic being. I considered him an old man, and beyond all that. A stubborn innocence seems to have been hard-wired into my thinking; in spite of all my exposure to psychotherapy and my youthful promiscuity, I persisted far later than most people in cluelessness about the role of sexuality in human motivation.

It was the Farber family that drew me even more powerfully than the talk of the salon that met irregularly at their apartment. It was the peace of a family dinner at their table, a peace that reigned imperturbably over all the squabbles and tiresomeness that three energetic young children could be counted upon to create. It was the softening I saw in Dr. Farber's eyes when he looked at his children (they addressed him, charmingly, as "Father"). It was the sense that in this family, whatever its problems and complexities, everything was deeply and solidly all right, and also—as in all families—fragile, contingent, and precious. "What family life teaches us about time is that it goes," Dr. Farber wrote in a late essay, "—that what it brings or gives or permits, it also transforms or hardens or takes away."

In that same essay, "Family Reunion," he defined family life as "a passionate daily traffic in perishables." In the Farber's apartment, I watched the swirling and eddying of that traffic. I watched as Anne directed it, as she tirelessly encouraged and chastened and interrogated, as one drama after another was enacted in her kitchen—tears, angry storms, delighted discoveries, reconciliations, early attempts at jokes.

It was from the Farbers that I learned about family, its purposes, its inescapability, its centrality in any notion of a good life. Characteristically, it was Dr. Farber who taught me the distanced view, the family under the aspect of time. From Anne I learned about dailiness. When I remember her, surrounded by the blur of her young children, who are grown now and surrounded by children of their own, I think of the poem by Randall Jarrell called "Well Water."

. . . *And yet sometimes*
The wheel turns of its own weight, the rusty
Pump pumps over your sweating face the clear
Water, cold, so cold! you cup your hands
And gulp from them the dailiness of life.

Anne took care of me in New York. She fed me: I ate at least two dinners a week at her table, and many breakfasts too, on mornings after the nights when it got too late to contemplate taking the subway home. She clothed me: When I was too poor to buy a coat, she gave me an old one of hers. My kitchen was equipped with her cast-offs. She offered me all kinds of practical help, lending me money and referring me to a gynecologist and dispatching her oldest son, Luke, to help me when I moved into my new apartment; he and I took multiple uptown trips on the subway, carrying my possessions in boxes. He spent a Saturday afternoon with me prying layers of old linoleum off the floors of the hall and kitchen. In return, he got to keep all the loose change this archeological dig unearthed.

I remember bursting into tears one day when Anne opened the door to their apartment, collapsing into her arms and sobbing. I don't recall the reason; perhaps I had been jostled too roughly on the rush-hour subway. She sat me down at the kitchen table, gave me a cup of tea, and waited receptively while I composed myself and tried to talk. I think I said that New York was just too much for me, that it was too hard—something like this. Anne took my hands and engaged my eyes and said, "You're thriving. In your own odd way you're thriving." And she was right—at least half right. If it's possible to thrive and collapse simultaneously, I suppose this is what I was doing in New York.

I stuck it out in the East Village until my roommate and I

returned after a weekend in Stockbridge to find that the windows had been broken and the place ransacked. I left the city for a few months and went back to Washington, stayed with my parents, and took a typing course.

Before I left the city, Dr. Farber advised me to keep my emotional distance from my parents. Don't look to them for approval, he warned. That could kill you, he added. These were his exact words, and I remember feeling startled and a little puzzled by them.

My mother remarked on my pallor. I went to the dentist, bought some clothes, and slept for twelve hours at a stretch. The Farbers sent me a bottle of cognac for my birthday; I drank a small glass of it every night before bed. Dr. Farber replied to all my letters. I especially remember a passage in which he responded to my complaints about my father's behavioral tics at the dinner table. His own father, wrote Dr. Farber, had had a habit of sucking the marrow out of chicken bones. When Dr. Farber, then a teenager, registered his vehement objections to this practice, his mother gently intervened: That's the best part of the chicken for your father, she explained. His father looked up briefly during this exchange, Dr. Farber wrote, and then returned, all the more vigorously, to his sucking. Never in all eternity, Dr. Farber wrote, will anything redeem this moment for either my father or me.

When I returned to New York, I moved uptown. My new apartment, for which I paid all of sixty dollars rent a month, was fairly roomy in a chopped-up way, but except for its front room, which had a large window looking out on Isham Street, it was very dark and made more so by the blue-green color of its walls. All the rooms, but especially the tiny dark bedroom, dominated by a large crucifix-shaped discoloration on the wall, were redolent of the pious widow who had lived there alone for forty years.

I knew this because the super told me. You're lucky, he said. You only get a bargain like this when somebody dies. He was a big friendly black man who dropped by frequently. He always refused my invitations to come in, but as he stood at the door, his feet rooted on the tile of the hall, he braced one hand on the doorjamb and leaned so far into the apartment that by rotating his head he was able to survey the living room, the kitchen, and—if I had left the door open—the bedroom. Once he noticed a can of paint I had left in the hall. "I see you're a fixing-up young lady," he remarked approvingly.

Briefly, I was. After Luke Farber and I had pried off the old linoleum, my brother took the bus from Baltimore, where he was working as a conscientious objector, emptying bedpans in a hospital, and the two of us spent a weekend sanding and staining the floors. It was midsummer, I remember, and we had a happy, sweaty time together, drinking beer and working until well after dark, then walking out into the night coolness and taking a turn through Fort Tryon Park.

Before Andy's visit, I had felt a little like an intruder in this remote neighborhood, as yet uncolonized by the young and hip, so far uptown that its air seemed rarefied. With its meandering residential streets and squat gray apartment buildings with deep, shadowed courtyards, Inwood was reminiscent of a slightly grim quarter in some European city—Brussels? Berlin? Its main commercial artery, bustling Dyckman Street, lined with fabric and notions stores and fruit stands where women in kerchiefs haggled with vendors over the price of bruised pears, had an exotically parochial aspect. I had never lived entirely alone before, and the streets of Inwood seemed as foreign to me as any place I had ever been, but my forays with Andy to the hardware store and the Chinese take-out on Dyckman made them feel more navigable. The two of us accomplished our errands with a confidence and purpose I knew I could never muster on my own. When I had walked Andy—who, in his absence, I rarely thought of and always loved—to the El and seen him off on Sunday afternoon, I returned to my apartment, flung myself on my bed, and wept, overwhelmed by the purest, most intense loneliness I had ever felt.

In the weeks that followed, I borrowed a ladder and a drop-cloth from Mr. Brown and made a start on painting the front room, the one with the view of Isham Street. I painted every night after work, listening to scratchy top-ten hits on the transistor radio Andy had given me, and by the end of the week I had managed to complete three walls. Then, for some reason, my project stalled, and that stall became institutionalized; the ladder and dropcloth stayed where they were, not just for weeks but for more than a year. It was only much later, after I first began to see the man who would eventually become my husband, that I pried the hardened brush off the top of the paint can, washed it out, and began again.

The super's three young sons awaited me when I came home from work. They hid under the stairs in the lobby, watching me while I collected my mail—what there was of it—and as I climbed the stairs I heard their voices. "Hoo, hoo," they softly called out, "White Owl! White Owl!" Not until I happened to notice a box of White Owl cigars at the tobacco store on Dyckman Street did I understand the reference. They were comparing me to the White Owl girl, in her feathered owl-cap, and when I took an objective look at my home-made haircut in the bathroom mirror, I could see why.

I had fully expected to be fired from my job at Columbia, and one day a few months after I moved into my Inwood apartment, I was. I worked briefly as a temp, alphabetizing insurance claims made on behalf of people who had died in dentists' chairs under nitrous oxide, then found a job in midtown as a tape cataloguer at Recording for the Blind. I was fired there too, and moved on to a job manning a switchboard in the Empire State Building in the offices of a boys' clothing manufacturer. I was made to understand from the beginning that a new, automated phone system was due to be installed in six months, after which the company would no longer require me.

This was an ideal job. I was able to sit behind the board, shielded from the eyes of my immediate supervisor, and read novels all day. I never quite learned how to operate the system, and I disconnected many a call between the New York offices and the southern factories where the boys' pants were manufactured, but I felt secure in the certainty that nobody would bother to fire me when my tenure was so short.

When I grew tired of reading, I watched. The intrigues of the secretaries were diverting; they used me as an aside-catcher, as if the office were a stage and I was a prompter seated in the wings. The four of them were eternally feuding, and as they passed my station, they signaled their exasperation with one another to me, tossing their heads and rolling their eyes in my direction. The salesmen were a jolly, boorish, bibulous bunch, with their wide ties and mutton-chop sideburns. They were forever going to and coming back from lunch, and their peevish wives were forever calling from Long Island to track them down. They traveled in a pack, singing "Jeremiah Was a Bullfrog", boogie-walking through the outer office, snapping their fingers and winking at me conspiratorially as they went out the door.

The only other nonaligned person in the office was the boss himself, the man who had hired me — largely out of sympathy, I'm sure — a decent, conscientious, worried person. He had a habit of pacing in and out of his office, and when our eyes met, we smiled.

Every afternoon as I got on the uptown subway, I wrestled with the same decision: Would I stay on the train all the way to my stop and trudge up the stairs to my apartment where legions of cockroaches were preparing to scuttle at the flick of the light switch? Or would I yield to the temptation to spend another evening at the Farbers?

About half the time I managed to lash myself to the subway pole and stay on until my 211th Street stop. On my way home from the subway, I ducked into the small Italian deli just below the El and bought my standard dinner, liverwurst and marinated red peppers on rye bread and a container of chocolate milk. I ate this curled up on the couch in the three-quarters-painted front room with the window looking out on Isham Street. I owned only three other pieces of furniture — my bed, a canvas butterfly chair, and a small wrought-iron table with an octagonal marble top.

I watched TV while I ate; or at least I watched TV until the TV was stolen, as every electrical object I owned eventually was. I spent the rest of the evening sitting in the butterfly chair and looking out on Isham, smoking and reading, or just musing.

Occasionally I had a visitor, usually my cousin Dick. He entered silently and paced the apartment for a few hours, muttering and scattering ashes. I found his presence disconcerting at first, but as the months went by I began to ignore him; the two of us behaved as if we were characters in some absurdist play — me in my seat at the window, my back to Dick as he went on his short-

leash walkabout, conducting a sotto voce debate between the war-
ring voices in his head.

Other times it was my downstairs neighbor Anton. When I saw
his face in the peephole, I knew I was in for a strenuous evening; he
would be looking for a long, intimate talk, and the visit would not
end before he had told me how special I was and made a soulful pass
at me. Anton was a short, powerfully built former speed freak from
City Island. He lived in a ground-floor apartment with his girlfriend
and another couple. This was a group of quasi hippies, all from blue-
collar backgrounds, who saw themselves as urban homesteaders,
Inwood pioneers. They had done extensive work on their apartment,
converted it from a set of lonely, historically echoing rooms to an
elaborately cozy, softly lit communal den where the four commu-
nards sat in overstuffed armchairs—which they had found on the
street, Anton told me, and reupholstered themselves—eating
hashish brownies and playing hearts. I spent several evenings with
them, surveying their place enviously, feeling simultaneously grateful for their friendliness and profoundly out of my element.

Here was countercultural domesticity, another strand in the
braid of the 1960s. I appreciated the genuine warmth with which
Anton and his roommates welcomed me, but there was something
both smug and dismayingly provisional about their ingeniously
improvised household that no amount of *Whole Earth Catalog*
resourcefulness could conceal. Once, when I had accepted the joint
that was passed to me, I looked at the faces of Anton and his roommates, shadowed and mottled by the candlelight, and was seized by
the disordered idea that they were more elfish than human, or rather
that they were human beings in the process of becoming elves. This
was what the counterculture was about, wasn't it? Anything was
acceptable but complex and problematic human nature: Elves,

sprites, animals, gods, demigods—these were the forms into which
the members of my generation willed themselves to morph.

This was not a new thought for me, but in my stoned state it took
on a crazy literal-mindedness. An image sprang into my head, an
endless warren of underground chambers, connected by a tortuous
system of tunnels and crawlways. It was in one of the most remote of
these little caves that I felt I had found myself now, in the company
of four veteran den-dwellers whose coziness had turned alien and
threatening. It seemed to me that I might be both trapped and lost
forever, that I might never find my way back to the central place, the
room that communicated with the surface. I got up and left in a
panic, apologizing incoherently as Anton's concerned girlfriend followed me to the door. When I had returned to my own chilly, bare
rooms, I was overwhelmed with relief at my escape.

The central place was not my apartment, of course, but the Farbers'. Two or three evenings a week I lost my battle with myself
and got off the subway at 110th Street. The light and warmth and
bustle of the Farber household were irresistible, and so was the
prospect of the welcome I would get from Anne and the children.

But I was wearing out that welcome, and I knew it. The more
time I spent there, the more I began to sense that Dr. Farber was dis-
pleased with something, perhaps with me. Often in the late afternoons I would sit in the kitchen at the table with one or two of the
children while Anne stood at the stove sautéing onions, overseeing
the children's homework, and talking intensely with me. Dr. Farber
would come into the room rather stiffly, make himself an old-
fashioned—he drank exactly one of these every evening before dinner—and walk out, with no remark. Sometimes Anne went on with
her several occupations, quite oblivious to him, but on other occa-

sions she stopped and watched him as he retreated through the kitchen door, her hands on her hips and an expression of consternation on her face. The children registered this: I saw them look up.

Sometimes there was a tension between the Farbers, moments when Anne's theatrical intensity seemed to offend and estrange him, even to drive him out of the apartment for a solitary walk on Broadway. I sensed that this tension was an ongoing one in their marriage, and had nothing directly to do with me, but I also wondered whether my presence was sometimes the occasion for it.

Once, a week or so before Christmas, I made a project of constructing a gingerbread house with the Farber children. I spent the afternoon doing the foundational work, the mixing of the gingerbread and the baking, and the early evening assembling and decorating the house with Dr. Farber's daughter Phoebe. But soon she grew tired of this project, and it was her bedtime anyway, so I was left in the kitchen, working doggedly into the night, studding the roof of the house with jelly beans, constructing a rough chimney from pieces of broken chocolate and peppermint sticks, my hands, clothes, and hair growing sticky with the white frosting I used as mortar. Dr. Farber sat at the table, smoking his Camels, watching the process with weary amusement, teasing me about my willful insistence on finishing this battered thing, which was already canting to one side and threatening to collapse.

Eventually I gave up; it must have been close to midnight. Dr. Farber escorted me to the door, and I remember how exhausted he looked as he stood waiting with me for the elevator. Years later it occurred to me that his motive in sitting up with me was not simple politeness—though it was certainly partly that. I think he was also doing something more primitive, something like guarding his home and family from an interloper.

*   *   *

Very early every Saturday, I took the train to Dr. Farber's office building on 103rd Street and Riverside Drive. I can distinctly remember the walk from the subway on Broadway on a brisk, clear winter morning, the dry snow creaking under my shoes and my eyes squinting and tearing in the wind and bright sun. The city was so quiet, so muffled by snow, that a flock of pigeons coming in for a landing in Riverside Park flapped thunderously over my head. It was impossible not to feel exhilarated on a morning that made the city seem so reborn, but I also remember how grubby and vulnerable I felt, how tired and unwell and full of excited anticipation and nonspecific dread.

Dr. Farber had a corner office, very high up, with a small kitchen and two rooms looking down on Riverside Park and across the Hudson. I remember him as he opened the door to his office, stepping slightly to one side to allow me to pass. He wore a plaid shirt and a corduroy jacket. The brown and white streaks of the river hung behind him; his face was tired in the morning light, his jowls heavy, his expression courteous and a little veiled.

Once seated, we talked about movies, books, some of the members of the cast of characters who showed up at the Farbers' soirees. These conversations were not unlike our talks at Riggs, except that at Riggs they had sometimes magically slipped into the realm of real dialogue. Now that no longer seemed to happen; as the months passed I was more and more self-conscious facing Dr. Farber, straining more and more desperately to keep him amused. To my own ears, my words sounded stilted, falsely animated. The more desperately I willed relation to return, the more stubbornly, of course, it refused my overtures.

I only half acknowledged the failure of these talks, but to the degree that I did, I sensed vaguely there was something new and wrong with the way I was positioned. At Riggs, both Dr. Farber and I had been able to look out together at the common world of the institution. But here in New York, my psychic home was Dr. Farber's apartment. My own apartments, my jobs, the world of my existence—all these were anterooms to that central place. I felt I could not reach into this territory that was essentially his, and private, without invitation, and so I found myself once again paralyzed by passivity.

I could not help being aware of the grotesque disjunction between the apparent playfulness and sophistication of my conversational offerings in Dr. Farber's office and the reality of my New York existence. The struggles of my daily life—getting to work on time under threat of being fired, making it to the laundromat, forcing down my terror of crime, and trying to stay clean when the hot water in my building was more often off than on—these were things I felt free to talk about with Anne, but not with Dr. Farber. I was too anxious to impress him, too fearful of boring him.

And gradually, for long stretches of time, I began to stop talking entirely. This phenomenon filled me with dread, and I remember sitting in Dr. Farber's chair, my head turned away from him, my hand shielding my face, silently mouthing the shapes of speech. I became aphasic, much as I had when I sat in the darkened bedroom of the ailing famous theologian. Dr. Farber's throat clearings and position shiftings made me wince and grind my teeth with panicky embarrassment, and so did the sequence of small sounds he produced with his boxy metal cigarette lighter—the miniature clank as it opened on its hinge, the scratch and the whir as it lit.

Perhaps if I had had a larger intellectual reservoir to draw upon, things might have been different. But the poverty of my education was beginning to catch up with me now; it had been so radically incomplete that I had grown up to be a creature of hunches and blurts, and soon even these had dried up. My sketchy views had long since been outlined and exhausted, and all I had to give back to Dr. Farber were flimsily disguised recapitulations of his own.

As dialogue failed, adulation flourished. George Eliot, in a reference to phrenology, the psychology of her day, once spoke of her oversized "Organ of Veneration." Apparently I had one too. I became a furtive taxonomist, dividing the world into the Farberian and the non-Farberian. What was Farberian I would embrace; what was non-Farberian I would reject.

But sometimes—frequently—I got it wrong. Once I told Dr. Farber that I wanted to explore orthodox Judaism. What I knew of his tightly guarded belief in God and his interest in Martin Buber gave me confidence that this would please him. Dr. Farber looked at me with amused incredulity. You want to wear a wig? he asked me. You want to take a ritual bath every month? Seriously?

Anne, with her sympathy and generosity, readily expanded to fill up the space between Dr. Farber and me. For this I was very grateful, because I found the distance painful. But her concern and care for me had the entirely unintended consequence of making it impossible for me to reach him.

She began to take on an intercessory role. Once, for example, soon after I had resumed my therapy with Dr. Farber, I began to notice that his behavior toward me had become not only remote but distinctly chilly. I panicked. Unable to bring myself to confront Dr. Farber, I asked Anne if she had any guesses about what might be bothering him. She questioned me: Might I be reading something into his customary reserve? No, I said; this was different. After a few moments of silent puzzling, she turned to me with widened eyes and a look of alarm. Emily, she asked, have you paid?

Paid? I asked blankly.

His *fee*, she said. He expects to be paid his fee. Stunned by my own idiocy, I smote my forehead with my palm. The truth was it had never occurred to me.

Dr. Farber accepted my apology graciously, and when I stammered something about not being able to pay in full, he assured me he would accept a payment proportionate to my income. Together, we worked out an amount I could afford—seven dollars and fifty cents a session.

Daniel was another of the three Riggs patients who had followed Dr. Farber to New York, an intellectually promising and sensitive young man with a yeshiva background. Like me, he had spent several years languishing at Riggs, his prognosis growing steadily worse, before Dr. Farber rescued him.

Daniel had resumed his interrupted education at Columbia, and during the time I worked there, I often ran into him on Broadway, at Chock full o' Nuts, and in the bookstores. We talked sometimes on the phone, and though we were not intimate, we maintained a concern for one another's fortunes in the city, a kind of loose sibling connection.

For a year or so Daniel stayed on the dean's list, but then something gave way in his life, and he began to skip classes. Eventually, he dropped out. During one of our phone conversations, he sheepishly confided that he had withheld this news from Dr. Farber. I felt a frisson of excited horror at this confession. How do you get around it? I asked, with a certain professional curiosity. I more or less avoid the subject, said Daniel, and changed the subject.

Time passed, and Daniel continued the deception. I began to feel obscurely troubled by my knowledge, to feel an urge to off-load it, and during one of our cozy late-night chats, I mentioned it to Anne. She immediately passed the information along to Dr. Farber, who confronted Daniel during his next session. I learned a few days later from Daniel that he had been, as he put it, "thrown out" of his therapy. Thrown out? I asked. Not exactly, he admitted. It was more like a mutual agreement.

I went to my next Saturday morning session glowing with schadenfreude. On the subway I prepared myself to plead Daniel's case. I wanted to remind Dr. Farber about Daniel's history, the oppressively high expectations of his parents, the over-shadowing intellectual success of his older brother.

But my first glance at Dr. Farber ended that fantasy. When he opened the door to his office, he looked steadily at the floor, and when we were seated and I had launched into some preliminary stammering, he raised his eyes to mine with such disgust and anger that I fell silent. I saw now how exhausted and ill he looked, as if he had not slept adequately for days. "How could you . . ." he began, then shook his head and fell silent. I was already weeping.

When he spoke again, Dr. Farber's voice was low and hoarse, his speech discontinuous, as if he were vocalizing only random chopped-off segments of thought. But I got the idea. I had colluded with a deception, and that had compromised my friendship with Dr. Farber, and my whisperings to Anne had in turn contaminated, if only briefly, his marriage. "How could you come into my home," he asked, "and . . . solicit . . . my wife?"

I had meanwhile pitched myself out of my chair onto my knees. Panic and grief had transported me, broken up a complex internal logjam. This moment was shocking, but it arrived with a satisfying sense of inevitability. For months I had been dangling, stretching my toes to feel for the bottom, and at last I had been delivered the judgment I had been dreading and craving. Suddenly I found I was able to speak fluently and from my heart. Please forgive me, I said. I had forgotten. Or perhaps I never learned.

Never learned what? asked Dr. Farber.

That things matter, I said, and for the first time since I had entered his office, he looked at me as if I were a fellow human being. Yes, they do, he said.

I understood that I had gotten it wrong, unconsciously slipped back to the precepts of my early therapeutic education. I had reverted to thinking of the relationship between Dr. Farber and Daniel, between Dr. Farber and me, as a game played for therapeutic chips, not as a reality in which a community of human connection was at stake.

But of course Dr. Farber had gotten it wrong too—I think now—because my silence on the subject of Daniel's deception had as much to do with simple reluctance to be a snitch as it did with any larger failure to honor human relatedness. I realize now that the most powerful motivator in my collusion with Daniel's dishonesty had been my impulse toward solidarity with another adolescent in the face of adult authority. My behavior had been stupid and callow, but essentially innocent.

Perhaps I should have defended myself against Dr. Farber's misdirected anger, which shocked me so much that I was unable to assimilate its meaning. But in fact I welcomed his explosion. It was relief at the exposure of a much deeper guilt—guilt at my own bad faith, at my collapse into dependency, at my desperate clutching at a friendship I knew had ended—that found expression in my tearful contrition.

By the end of the hour, I felt that Dr. Farber had offered me a kind of amnesty. He waved me out of his office with an air of pre-occupied disgust, but I could sense that in his exasperation, his sense of humor had wanly reasserted itself. Before I left, I won from him the assurance that I could return the next week.

I envied Daniel the seriousness of his transgression. I suspected that Dr. Farber cared more about him than he did about me; his anger was like a father's toward a beloved errant son. And like an errant son, Daniel had been cut decisively free; he left New York and moved to Israel, joined the army, and married there, returning to the States years later with his young family. His dismissal from Dr. Farber's office left him bereft, but it also served to jolt him out of a rut. He got to keep, it seemed to me, some of his legacy from Dr. Farber, whereas my lesser, weaker, more equivocal offense kept me tied to Dr. Farber for another year, during which I was using mine up.

Or so I understood myself to be doing. But in the meantime I found yet another job, serving as the amanuensis of an elderly and hypochondriacal avant-garde composer who dictated his memoirs to me in the study of his overheated Riverside Drive apartment. I also met and eventually moved in with the man who was to become my husband. George was then a graduate student in philosophy at Columbia, very bright, analytical, and skeptical, and though he was five years my senior, he was also, like me, very young for his age. He took a satirical view of my attachment to Dr. Farber, comparing me to a character in one of R. Crumb's underground comic books—the goofy, loose-limbed Flakey Foont, always in pursuit of his guru Mr. Natural, an irascible little visionary with a long white beard and giant flapping bare feet.

One night, after I had returned from a walk with a friend along

Broadway and was fumbling in my purse for my keys in the entranceway to the 108th Street brownstone apartment building where George and I lived, I was accosted by two teenaged boys and raped at knifepoint in the hallway. Soon after this I began a campaign, and not a subtle one, to persuade George that we needed to get married as soon as possible.

A few months before my wedding, I ended my therapy with Dr. Farber. I confessed to him that I had had little to say to him for years. I needed to leave, I told him, because I was in danger of becoming the acolyte who gets the master's message wrong. I knew how little Dr. Farber wished to serve as my guru, and I knew how particularly inappropriate my idealizing impulse toward him was. His tendency was deflationary: He nearly always preferred a modest exactitude to a rapturous generality.

I can see myself, I told him, twenty years from now as a barfly, the regular who climbs onto her stool every afternoon at two and by four o'clock is mumbling to anybody who will listen the incoherent tale of the wise man she once knew in her youth. Dr. Farber accepted my resignation with real warmth. My confession was true, and he liked it because it was true, and because it had a self-immolating boldness calculated to appeal to him. I offered it not only because it was true, but also because it was the only way I knew to please him.

George and I were married in Williamstown in the summer of 1972. My parents had recently bought a house there for summer use and, they hoped, their eventual retirement. The wedding was a hastily pulled together late afternoon affair, with rows of chairs set up on the lawn in the shade of a catalpa tree, looking out on uncropped fields and the encircling Berkshire mountains.

My husband memorably described our wedding as a "barely civil ceremony." He and I had had a shouting fight that kept us up most of the night before, and he looks rather dazed in the photographs. His parents appear in the pictures too, stiff and a little stricken, seated with my parents and other wedding guests on the flagstone patio. Looking through the pictures, I see myself in my dress of terra cotta Mexican cotton and my ill-judged floppy pink hat, cutting the cake and receiving presents. In many of the pictures, I notice that I'm holding my right wrist with my left hand, as if I were unconsciously restraining that arm from some Strangelovian rebellion. I was doing this because, under pressure from George, I had for the first time given up smoking, something I would attempt perhaps thirty times over the next twenty years before I finally succeeded. In a few shots, my expression is oddly sidelong and confiding, as if I were sending a message to the later self who would look at these photographs.

Here's another photograph, showing my Aunt Helen and my paternal grandmother. I notice how bony and bowed my grandmother's legs had become, even as her torso had thickened. This seems to be a familial aging pattern; I saw the same change in my father, and I can see it beginning to happen to me. Both ladies are sitting in state on flimsy lawn chairs in the leafy shade of the catalpa tree on this lovely summer afternoon, holding cold drinks in clear glasses, their elderly ankles crossed. I see Caroline, looking more like a bridesmaid, in her long dress, than I looked like a bride. I see other aunts and uncles and family friends, my sister and her then-husband and their small son. I see my mother, looking so harried that there are specks of froth at the corners of her mouth, and my newly slender father—his cardiologist had put him on a draconian diet—escorting me down the aisle between the banks of rented chairs toward the catalpa tree and the town clerk.

Both my parents are dead now, of course, as are many of the relatives who attended this wedding, and some of the friends. Perhaps a third of the people in these photographs are gone, and looking through them has put me in a surprisingly elegiac frame of mind— surprising because a harshly dismissive attitude toward my parents and their world has become so habitual to me. But what I feel is really rather impersonal—a large, pleasant, wondering sadness. So much time has passed; this is my simple and unoriginal thought.

To feel these emotions and think these thoughts is satisfying and reassuring to me, because they are so exactly appropriate for a person my age. The ceremony recorded in my wedding pictures was hastily improvised, but the marriage has lasted, and these pictures have become historical. Time has anchored and stabilized this marriage that began so unhappily and inauspiciously. It has continued for twenty-seven years, growing stronger by fits and starts, and one of its late-arriving rewards has been a steadiness that makes the past transparent, a pool so clear and still that I can see all the way to its bottom. "Children are born," wrote Dr. Farber in his essay "Family Reunion," "they grow, they grow up, they go away from us toward their own lives, our own parents die, our friends die, it is growing late, it is years since we began."

Anne was present at my wedding too, and her daughter Phoebe, who looked so charming in her blue calico dress that I impulsively pressed her into service as my flower girl. Dr. Farber did not attend.

7

MY LAST THERAPIST

Twelve years after I exiled myself from Dr. Farber, I first shook hands with Dr. B, my last therapist. I was living in a small New England city where my husband taught at the state university. Our daughter was eighteen months old, and I had just put her in part-time day care and returned to the project of completing the master's degree in English I had abandoned in the seventh month of my pregnancy.

Dr. B was the first therapist I sought out by myself. I remained his patient for seven years, a longer time than I spent with any of his five predecessors. He was the first therapist I engaged as an adult, and he was the first, I think it's fair to say, who represented a mainstream, middle-of-the-road psychotherapeutic perspective. Perhaps it is more accurate to say he was the first of my therapists whose methods a mainstream, middle-of-the road psychotherapist would find unexceptionable. With Dr. B, I believe I saw psychotherapy subjected to a reasonably fair test.

Thinking about him now, visualizing his office, I see myself slightly hunched at one end of his comfortable leather couch. I see him flung back in his specially designed orthopedic rocker, his corduroy-sheathed legs outstretched, his ankles crossed, his bald pate gleaming. I see the two of us looking out from our lamp-lit island into a parcel of shadowy office space, in the direction of the darkened alcove where Dr. B typed up his bills and displayed photographs of his wife and children that, squint and peer and crane my neck as I might, I could never quite make out.

This is Dr. B's second office I'm picturing, the one he moved into six months after I became his patient, when he severed his connection with the university hospital. He rented space in a newly renovated downtown building because he felt the hospital bureaucracy was insensitive to his patients' need for confidentiality. It distressed him to ask them to wait in a holding area shared by people in hospital gowns waiting to be x-rayed.

He was a fit and pleasant-looking man in his early forties, just enough my elder for comfort, with a rather long and slightly horsey face, a little like Prince Charles's, or a Semitic version of John Updike's. His handshake was a good omen—a firm grasp, two hard pumps, and a clean release. He emanated sensitivity and goodwill, and he had a fine speaking voice, an anchorman's baritone, which tended to lighten as he grew animated. By the time our acquaintance was five minutes old, I had formed an opinion of him that I never entirely abandoned, though I did revise and expand it: ordinary. He was the good-enough therapist.

In order to find Dr. B, I had done a considerable amount of investigation. Our university town was lousy with therapists; there must have been at least a hundred, of every variety, from the Rolfers and rebirthers who advertised in the local alternative paper to highly credentialed analysts whose clientele lived in houses overlooking the lake. Before I settled down with Dr. B, I eliminated— or was eliminated by—four other practitioners.

I began by consulting a psychiatrist, a stiff, fussy older man. I've long since forgotten who recommended him. I recognized him from the synagogue, where I had attended Saturday morning services when I was considering an official conversion in the months before my daughter's birth. He and several other elderly regulars in yarmulkes and prayer shawls had craned their necks to stare at me suspiciously as I stood among the congregants, hugely pregnant and unescorted. (My husband wanted nothing to do with any religious observance.) When I showed up at his office he showed no sign of reciprocal recognition, but I could tell right away that he disliked me. "Farber," he said, when I began to speak about Dr. Farber. "I don't think I'm familiar with any Farber." He rose laboriously from his chair and shuffled to his desk, where he sat down with a sigh, turned on a tensor lamp, put on his reading glasses, and paged through a directory of psychoanalysts. "Farber, Herbert," he murmured. "Farber, Jonathan. Farber, Karl. Ah yes, Leslie Farber." He glanced up at me balefully; it seemed I could not be dismissed as delusional.

Next was a psychologist who worked in the counseling department at the university. She wore a long batik skirt and reverse-gravity Mary Janes. We sat facing one another in twin wooden rocking chairs in a room so festooned with plants that the air itself seemed to be tinged with green. She listened to my long, confused, rambling self presentation—Riggs, Farber, New York, my marriage—with grave and gentle attention, and when I finally ground to a halt, she asked me if I had regular orgasms.

I moved on to an intense, youngish psychiatrist with an abrupt manner and a quick, flashing, predatory smile. As I walked down the cobblestone mews to the rear entrance of his architect-designed building, I noticed a brilliantly polished antique Jaguar parked just by the door. This therapist met me as I was coming in, ushered me into his cathedral-ceilinged therapy room, and seated me in a chair some twenty feet from his, so distant that we both had to half shout in order to be heard. He did this, he explained, because he was interested to learn what a patient's body had to say; the nervous tapping of a foot could give him reams of information.

He perused one of several forms he had sent me when I called for the consultation. " A lot of therapy," he observed. "Maybe too much therapy." I asked him if this meant that I had shot my wad, and that more therapy would only do me harm. "No, no," he said. "I mean it's high time somebody did it right." Once again I began my spiel—by now I had begun to feel like a character in a fairy tale: Would one of these therapists be able to answer the qualifying riddle?—but as I talked, I was distracted by an intrusive thought. Just the night before, while talking to a friend on the phone, I had mentioned that I planned to consult this doctor. My friend burst into laughter. I know that guy, she said. His son's in our school carpool. Every single time he does the driving, he comes into our house, helps himself to a section of the paper, and shits in our guest bathroom.

Finally, or penultimately, I consulted a senior psychiatrist who practiced in the local hospital. This man was leaving the profession (in disgrace, I later learned. He was an out-of-control alcoholic). His office was full of packed boxes, its air thick with cigarette smoke.

He was a dejected-looking character with nicotine-stained teeth and a distracting tremor—a ruined man, it seemed to me, but also a human being. He was the only one of the four therapists I interviewed whom I liked. He reminded me, faintly but distinctly, of Dr. Farber—I sensed a little of the same gravity and vulnerability behind his air of rank defeat. Partly because of this recognition, and partly because he was leaving the profession, I felt inclined to confide in him. I sat down, burst into tears, and told him about the fights my husband and I had been having. We had been doing so much better, I said, but now we were shouting at each other again.

He listened quietly, and after I had pulled myself together, he wrote down three names on a piece of paper and passed it to me. These people are all fine, he said. All well qualified. Can you give me a sense of the order in which you recommend them, I asked. The doctor paused for a moment, shrugged, and gave me a gallant, hopeless smile. (Here was a man Dr. Farber would have recognized as a despairer.) No, he said, they're all perfectly fine.

Dr. B was the first of those perfectly fine therapists to return my call. As we spoke on the phone, I found myself drawn by the warmth and energy in his voice. When I mentioned that I was interested in writing, he told me he had a special interest in working with writers and artists. He was the only one of all the therapists I consulted who passed the Farber-recognition test. He had read a few of Dr. Farber's essays and noticed his obituary in the *New York Times.* "Irreplaceable," Dr. B said, "lifesaving," and I loved him for that.

But then, during our first session, he went on to link Dr. Farber with my father, who had died seven years earlier. "A lot of loss," he said, shaking his head deploringly. I felt for the first time the prickly irritation and the faint vertigo that would become such familiar sensations in the years to follow as I sat on Dr. B's couch, symptoms of the imperfect sympathy between us. He had said something almost but not quite right, and I was uncomfortably balanced between the impulse to point that out to him and a desire to leave well enough alone. I didn't like the idea of packaging Dr. Farber and my father together, but I let it pass.

Perhaps I should have been more vigilant, because a few sessions later, he said something almost unforgivable. He interrupted one of my anecdotes about Dr. Farber with what he called "a reality consideration." Dr. Farber had certainly been a marvelous and very unique therapist, he said. (Again I bit my tongue and stifled an impulse to correct him, this time on his misuse of the word "unique.") But Farber had also been well known in the profession as a sufferer from depression. Was it possible, Dr. B conjectured, that during my years as Dr. Farber's patient, I had tried to compensate him for his sadness, just as I had done with my unhappy mother?

How many things, I thought, could be wrong with this approach? Could anything be right? First, the "reality consideration": Was it implied here that the profession had a corner on reality? And depression: Dr. Farber had his own views on depression. I suggested to Dr. B that he go to the library and look them up. What the profession took to be Dr. Farber's depression was actually despair.

But I was too angry to argue; instead I picked up the first wad of ad hominem that came to hand and flung it in Dr. B's direction. I looked up at the framed photograph of a sinking ship that Dr. B displayed on his wall—the deck drastically tilted and swamped with seawater—and this put me in mind of an analogy; I compared Dr. Farber to an ocean-going liner with a great deep hull, and Dr. B to a surface-skimming sailfish. Two spots of bright pink appeared just below Dr. B's cheekbones, and I pointed them out to him, literally pointed with my finger, all the while registering in one corner of my mind the appalling rudeness of the gesture.

I was working myself into a rage, and I could see that Dr. B was calculating how best to backtrack and calm me down. He threw up his hands. Okay, he said. You're quite right. I was out of line. I'm not perfect. Do you need me to be perfect?

No, I said. I need you to be smart. Dr. B absorbed that without comment, and we sat in silence for several minutes. I was registering my disgust at the hokeyness of the "I'm not perfect" line and the seductive pseudo-intimacy of "do you need me . . . ?" I was also fuming at the realization that Dr. B had saved his remarks about Dr. Farber until he had me well roped in as a patient. He had waited until it seemed safe to introduce his revisionist agenda. He was getting off, no doubt, on the idea of rescuing me from my thralldom to a distinguished dead practitioner. This was the supplanter's story so familiar to the profession.

Here I was, seated in the office of my sixth therapist. Hadn't I decided, with Farber's help and long ago and repeatedly, that what I needed was to recover *from* therapy? What, then, was I doing here?

One thing I was *not* doing was undertaking a revision of my views of Dr. Farber. I made it clear that this was a touchy subject, and Dr. B, as far as I can remember, never brought it up again. (He did make a few remarks: When I mentioned that Dr. Farber once suggested I substitute the word "flair" for "talent" when describing my writing aptitude, Dr. B murmured, "Always there to burst your bubble, wasn't he?")

Why, after my twelve-year boycott, did I go back into therapy? I was, if anything, doing far better at this point than I had for the first five or six years of my marriage. (Amazing how my lifelong exposure to secondhand psychoanalytic thought has limbered up my mind. Executing explanatory flips comes as second nature to me: If the idea of a desperate collapse into the arms of therapy doesn't quite consort with the historical facts, the notion of a revolution of rising expectation conveniently presents itself.)

Immediately after our marriage, my husband and I had moved from the Upper West Side to Leonia, New Jersey, a bedroom suburb two towns beyond the George Washington Bridge. We rented the top floor of a stodgy brown-and-white shingled house. I was relieved to be out of Manhattan—since my rape I had lost my city nerves—and my husband was happy to be free of the commute to the suburban New Jersey university where he taught. Our plan was that I would take the bus into the city and attend Columbia General Studies, but I had abandoned that enterprise within a few months. Instead, for two years I spent my days lying in bed, reading and chain-smoking. In the evenings I cooked elaborate dinners for my husband—he would have preferred less fuss, and something simple—and drank bourbon, a third of a bottle every night. Within six months of our wedding, my life with my husband had become a grotesque parody of my parents' marriage.

Except it lacked the civility that my parents showed each other. We fought so loudly and bitterly and constantly that the neighbors complained. I followed my husband through the apartment, shrieking and weeping and accusing. Sometimes he bellowed back at me—he was just as choleric as I, though more measured because less self-destructive. But more often he lowered his head and ducked into his study, locking the door behind him. This room was his only escape, he insisted. He was determined to write his way out of his current dead-end teaching job, and he required a modicum of peace in order to think clearly.

It was his failure to care about me that I taxed him with. It enraged me to watch him going doggedly about his business, as if I were a terrible given in his life, something to ignore whenever possible, and otherwise to work around. I taunted him with accusations of spinelessness. If you had an *inside* you'd leave me, I said. But you stay because you'd lose too much writing time. The two of us held one another in paralyzing check: I made our marriage ugly by smearing it with my rage and self-disgust; he put up with my behavior out of guilt over his selfishness and ambition.

When I run my memory over this period, I find that it feels different from other regions of my recollection—smooth and thick, like scar tissue. I imagine that people who have recovered from long illnesses remember, or misremember, them in a similar way.

When I described my Leonia years to Dr. B, he was quick to suggest post–traumatic stress, the sequela of my rape. I found this idea comforting but unilluminating, an instance of scientific relabeling, dignifying a bruise by calling it a hematoma.

Though I resisted the idea when I was his patient, I've come to accept Dr. B's more general retrospective diagnosis of depression. But at the same time, I believe that entwined with my depression was a quite distinct and far more ancient condition. I was depressed, certainly, but I had contracted another condition as well. I had finally attained to the peculiarly human and non-pathological state that Farber called despair.

Farber drew a detailed diagram of the machinations of despair in his essay "Despair and the Life of Suicide." I recognize my behavior in his description of the despairer who

> [d]esperately hungry for reconciliation . . . becomes increasingly estranged from those loved ones who might conceivably offer

him some relief, if it were not being demanded by him. At this stage in his deprivation, he may turn unhappily to the task of documenting his estrangement by becoming a self-appointed, though miserable, expert on those deficiencies in his fellows that render them incapable of love—particularly the love toward him that would lighten his despair.

Despair is intimately connected both to guilt and pride. My guilt—and here Farber would insist that I make explicit the distinction between guilt and guilt feelings—was incurred when, grieving the loss of Dr. Farber and unstrung by my rape, I extorted a marriage proposal from my husband, who feared that if he did not marry me he would lose me. There was much to mitigate the wrongness of what I did, but I compounded the original sin repeatedly by my angry persecution of my husband, my enraged and doubly impossible demand that he reassure me not only of his love for me but of my love for him as well.

The hard kernel at the center of my despair was my pride at having exiled myself from Dr. Farber. Even though I understood that a good part of my motive had been to protect myself from a dreaded rejection, I took a dark pleasure in what I saw as the spiritual glamour of that renunciation. This pride was the marker for my despair, its ally and supporter. The despairer, Dr. Farber wrote:

> experiences an overwhelming longing to confess—but what he confesses is not his wickedness, which would be a proper subject for confession and which might involve him in some redeeming attitude toward both his confession and his life. Instead, what he wishes to confess is his worthlessness—his infirmity. Such a confession is spurious, of course: it does not touch on issues of forgiveness or repentance that are relevant to his condition.

One of the hallmarks of despair is the despairer's conviction that he has found himself in a trap; having ruminatively and obsessively considered and ruled out every angle of escape, he refuses to acknowledge even the possibility that he might be released. In Leonia, I had engineered just such a diabolical trap for myself. On the one hand, by renouncing Dr. Farber, I had cut myself off from the only confessor who could hear my confession in moral rather than therapeutic terms. And just as surely, in my hopeless loyalty to Dr. Farber, I had dismissed the possibility of consulting anyone who might have offered me another kind of help.

One evening, after my husband and I had been living in Leonia for a year, a friend who was also a Farber patient called to tell me that Dr. Farber had suffered a stroke. When I called Anne, she reassured me that he could still walk and talk and that his mind was essentially intact, though for a while he had been very confused. On his first night in the hospital, she reported, he had gotten out of bed, shrugged off his hospital gown, and thinking he was in his own apartment, wandered naked down the hall. He caused a ruckus in the ward by getting in bed with an elderly man, who shrieked and flailed at him with his fists.

I was a little shocked at Anne's tone of grim amusement. I was still a soft and inexperienced creature; medical disaster was new to me, and I viewed Dr. Farber's stroke with sanctimonious terror. I was not yet able to appreciate the comforts of humor in these situations, and I found the mental image that this story called up horrifyingly sad.

I still do, I suppose, but I also find it oddly comforting to think of him that way. He was, after all, a human being, and in that condition—old, sick, confused, naked, wandering—he seems particularly and poignantly so. I understand now, with the benefit of long hindsight, that Dr. Farber may well already have been ill when he exploded at me over Daniel's deception. Neurologically ill, I mean, not psychologically—ill in a way that truly did excuse him from one degree or another of responsibility.

But, as Anne told me later, he was not so damaged by his stroke as to fail to see humor in the story about his nocturnal wanderings. He was able to return to his practice, and in spite of his capricious short-term memory—which was a great torture to him, Anne told me—he was also able to produce a few more essays, particularly deep and powerful ones. He even—and here was a true renunciation—gave up his cigarettes. After the stroke, he lived for eight more years.

In spite of my efforts at sabotage, my husband succeeded in writing his way to a better teaching job. We moved to New England; he taught and I studied, earning a B.A. and eventually an M.A. in English.

As they sometimes quite naturally do, things got somewhat better. When I went back to school, I found satisfaction in discovering that I suddenly seemed able to learn and excel academically. Gradually, the fights between my husband and me became less intense and frequent, and during the longer stretches of peace, we were able to cultivate the natural affinity we had felt for each other from the beginning. I began to write, short stories at first and then two misbegotten novels. My drinking—and surely I would have been diagnosed as an alcoholic if I had sought treatment when it was at its worst—spontaneously moderated itself.

One morning in 1980, when my husband and I were spending a sabbatical year in Chapel Hill, North Carolina, I came upon Dr. Farber's obituary in the *New York Times*. This news did not shock me; instead it put me into a subtly altered state, a deep musing calm that lasted all day and then mysteriously lifted. I took a long walk to the arboretum at the university, and as I sat among the blossoming cherry trees and magnolias, I reflected on Dr. Farber and his life in such a tranquil and orderly way that it seemed to me all the other channels in my mind had been cleared for the purpose.

In the early months with Dr. B, I assumed a new persona. I became hostile and prickly. I sneered at the nautical decor in his new office, especially the coffee table, which was a sheet of glass affixed to an old lobster trap. I took out after his ties, particularly a forest-green one printed with a repeating pattern of tiny mud boots and the logo "L. L. Bean."

My hostility toward this tie must have presented Dr. B with a problem. (How well I know this script!) Wearing it frequently on my therapy days would have amounted to a provocative gesture, but banishing it from his wardrobe entirely would have signaled a failure to impose appropriate limits, a capitulation that would have frightened me and plunged me into guilt by confirming my primitive fear that I could make my hostile wishes come true. He solved this clinical dilemma by wearing the tie regularly but infrequently—perhaps once every two months.

It's not lost on me that the sadistic and grandiose tendency of my behavior toward Dr. B was the mirror image of the masochistic self-abnegation I had shown Dr. Farber. I behaved unpleasantly because I was paying to behave any way I pleased, and because this was my emotionally primitive way of staying loyal to Dr. Farber. I was like a dog guarding the long-dead body of his master, snarling at anyone who approached.

I would never have felt free to be so nasty had I not been supremely confident of Dr. B's regard for me. It was, after all, overdetermined: Dr. B told me that his positive feelings toward me were highly useful to our work together, as were my negative feelings toward him. He explained that he could not will affection for a patient, but if he happened to feel it, he made sure to cultivate it for the sake of the therapy.

I took opportunistic advantage of this situation. The self I presented in Dr. B's office was so unlike my unassuming, polite, anxious-to-please usual self that anybody on the outside (except my husband) would have found it unrecognizable. And what could be better than this, a chance to behave as badly as I wished, to sit in sullen silence, to sneer, to make cutting remarks out of the corner of my mouth, while all the while Dr. B gazed at me like a doting, enlightened mother waiting out a child's tantrum? Surely, it occurred to me, I had something like this coming to me, spending my days, as I did, enduring my own child's tantrums. When I tried out this theory on Dr. B, he made an utterly predictable remark about how mothers need mothering, to which I responded by rolling my eyes.

This presentation of myself as a weary, put-upon mother was entirely and provocatively false. The fact was that I felt tremblingly grateful to have a child at all, awed, delighted, and amazed at her existence, convinced that her birth had given me a chance at a new, redeemed life, quite content to put up with any amount of two-year-old behavior. I envied the exasperation and exhaustion that other mothers complained about: Surely they would not have been capable of these attitudes if they had not integrated the reality of motherhood into their lives, as I seemed unable to do.

I had in fact developed something like a paranoid obsession

about the other mothers I observed at my daughter's part-time day care. They all seemed to exude confidence and competence; they went about the little jobs of child maintenance with an easy offhand grace. Under their eyes I became so ham-handedly self-conscious that I was unable to engage the zipper on my daughter's snowsuit, and I actually feared they were taking note of my clumsiness, whispering about me, questioning whether I was fit to care for a child.

I had (once again) become more than a little like Farber's despairer, to whom strangers passing on the street appear "transformed by their thoughtless possession of just what he has lost: the sheer, taken-for-granted ordinariness of life. In the misery of the envy they incite in him, he isolates and exalts that quality of life that can flourish only in disregard: a sense of belonging in whatever worlds one lives, a sense that is both concrete and casual." Having misrepresented myself in the service of a peevish demand for sympathy, and finding myself too enervated by spiritual nausea to retract my lie, I sat in silence for the rest of the session.

I've given a particularly extreme example of the fraudulence I was capable of when I sat on Dr. B's couch (from time to time he suggested I recline on it—I always refused). But it was typical of my sandbagging technique: I said something false about myself, allowed Dr. B to offer a tentative confirmation, and then slammed him for it. But, I reminded myself, as a patient I was entitled to indulge in this or any other kind of bad behavior, wasn't I?

Of course I enjoyed my sessions with Dr. B. In prospect, they were voluptuous, confectionary, a treat. In retrospect, they provided me with the pleasures of recollection, interpretation, and fantasy. Not since my early silent therapies had I felt such easy, passive pleasure. And there was a new element of excitement as well; a

courtship of sorts was going on in Dr. B's office. I heard and saw
an eagerness and ardor in his tone and expression that would have
been easy to mistake for erotic interest.

I understood it was not that. Instead it was something closely
allied to erotic interest—a collector's pleasure in a new acquisi-
tion. Dr. B was an ambitious and passionately committed professional—once he ruefully acknowledged that he had been accused
of having an addiction to doing therapy—and I could sense that
he considered me a prize. I could feel his desire to keep me as a
patient, his anxiety that he might lose me.

This was no fantasy; I had much to recommend me. I had literary leanings and aptitudes. I was bright, articulate, and (if only
recently) educated. I was sane, and free (again, if only recently) of
addictions. The circumstances of my life were stable and regular,
and I was still young enough to change. I had a sense of humor.
Even though I was only a graduate student/faculty wife, I had the
sociological cachet of a connection to the university. Surely I was
more sophisticated about psychotherapy than most of his other
patients—more fun too, if the snuffling and whining I overheard
while I sat in his waiting room were any indication. But what really
made Dr. B prize me as a patient, I believe, was that I had been
damaged, in his view, by an unconventional, failed therapy. I was
that irresistible thing—a reclamation project.

The reflection I saw in Dr. B's eyes was a flattering one, and I was
susceptible to flattery because my existence outside Dr. B's office
offered me little in the way of confirmation. Now that I had returned
to graduate study, I found my reign as an academic star was over; I
had taken so many years to complete my graduate course work that
I had become a half-forgotten curiosity in the English department.
As I inched my way through the program, I felt increasingly con-

stricted by the ever-narrowing focus of graduate-student scholarship. I discovered that my interest in literature was catholic rather than specialized, a writer's interest, not a scholar's.

The English department where I studied was provincial and fifth-rate, characterized by the most timid and sleepy kind of teaching and thinking. The whole enterprise of graduate study began to seem ridiculous to me, and I was overheard making impolitic remarks about some of my professors. Eventually I acquired a reputation for being odd and a little difficult, one of those characters on the fringes of academic life, viewed as gifted but uncategorizable and therefore not quite legitimate.

I had fallen from the state of grace that hovered around my daughter and me during her infancy. I had somehow managed to lose touch with most of my friends. My husband was deeply involved in writing a book, nearly as emotionally unavailable to me as he had been in Leonia. I was living an isolated, patched-together life, and as the months and years went by, I was visited with the eerie sensation that I was beginning to disappear. One reason I sought out Dr. B was quite simply that I was lonely.

Dr. B's attentions were sweet and seductive, and gradually the serious mock-hostility I manifested in his office changed its tone and became a playful mock-hostility. Dr. B responded with small knowing smiles, and soon we were engaged in Tracy-Hepburn style banter. We were playing a coy, flirtatious game. I was the pouting shrew, he the cajoling suitor. I loved it!

I began to have fantasies about Dr. B, long, implausible ones, embarrassingly derivative of disaster movies, romantic rather than explicitly erotic. They tended to dissolve into a pastel mist just at the point when real sexual fantasy would begin.

Here is the master scenario: Dr. B and I are having an after-hours session when a nuclear attack or an elevator cable severed through an act of sabotage maroons us in his top-floor office in the hospital. (I was and am fascinated by hospitals, and in my fantasies about Dr. B, the hospital was a major element. Perhaps I should say that in my fantasies about the hospital, Dr. B was a major element.)

We find ourselves alone together in his darkened office, trapped by circumstance. In some versions, nurses, interns, and medical students are buried in a pile of rubble at the other end of the hall where we can hear them calling faintly. Once or twice Dr. B and I heroically rescue them, but ordinarily my imagination balked at any complication that introduced a third party to the fantasy.

Isolation quickly breaks down our doctor-patient roles. In one frequently replayed fantasy, Dr. B is injured; his arm has been cut by flying glass, and I take charge by ripping a strip of fabric from the ugly institutional curtains and fashioning a makeshift tourniquet, which I apply to Dr. B's arm while he lies on the couch, pale, sweaty, and grimacing bravely. As Dr. B rests, I sit at his side, gently stroking his forehead. He falls asleep, and I go through his files, comparing the long, detailed, flattering notes he has kept on his sessions with me to his perfunctory scrawls about other patients. When he has recovered, we walk hand in hand through the deserted halls of the hospital.

In some versions, the tone shifts and becomes antic and risqué. Shrieking and laughing, we chase each other through empty laboratories; expensive glass tubes and beakers fall to the floor and smash in our wake. We clamber through the CAT-scan tunnel on our hands and knees, and the fantasy ends as we collapse on a gurney in an amorous heap.

Or, alternatively, the tone turns soft and serious. Dr. B and I sit in his office wrapped in one another's arms, gazing out at the poisoned dawn—we are soon to die of radiation poisoning.

I conscientiously reported all but the most embarrassing of these fantasies to Dr. B, who listened intently, taking notes as he did when I recounted a dream. When he asked me if these fantasies were ever overtly sexual, I had to confess, blushing at my backwardness, that they rarely were. I sensed that Dr. B was clinically disappointed in me, that I had failed a test of psychosexual maturity. I went home and applied myself to the task of imagining full sexual intercourse with Dr. B. I found that this was an exercise in paradox; the writhing male figure in my fantasy became instantly depersonalized. He was not Dr. B or any other real man, and so the purpose of my fantasy was defeated.

Dr. B kept his face in profile, his eyes lowered and shadowed. But he inclined his large listening ear toward me, and somehow he used that appendage expressively; something about its convoluted nakedness reassured and invited me. As the months and years passed, I realized he had a particular gift—how he had learned to do this I can't imagine—for conveying, simply by sitting there, a warm satisfaction in the fact of my existence. His body's attitude seemed to say, "you're quite something, all right!"

I had read enough about psychotherapy, absorbed enough through cultural osmosis, to understand that Dr. B was exercising a skill, practicing a technique. I knew about unconditional positive regard and mirroring and holding environments, and I also knew I was obliged to live with the knowledge that what transpired in Dr. B's office, however powerful its emotional charge, was not real. Dr. B was fond of saying that what went on between us was *very* real, but of course the intensifying "very" immediately threw up scare quotes around the "real."

From time to time, Dr. B seemed to struggle with the same cognitive dissonance that afflicted me. On one occasion, he mused aloud on the subject of "the real." Why, he asked rhetorically, were the emotions he felt in this room, which sometimes seemed far realer than anything he felt on the outside, somehow less legitimate? But then, of course, he remembered why, and also remembered that his professional life was posited upon this distinction. The puzzled look left his face; he shifted in his chair, and presented his ear to me once again.

When Dr. B expressed wonder or doubt, when he seemed to step briefly out of his role as therapist to join me in looking out at the system that engaged and trapped us both, I felt my cheeks flush with triumph. Surely it was my influence—my "specialness"—that had made him turn philosophical for a moment. And I indulged in the fantasy that I might actually prevail in the struggle going on between us, that instead of being led into the therapy world by Dr. B, I might lead him out.

But as the fantasy dissipated, I saw that Dr. B had won this round. It became clear he was the one who was leading—leading me on, in fact. His musings about the realness of his feelings were a calculated ploy, a quick flash of leg to keep me interested at a time when my doubts about therapy were getting the upper hand.

And if somehow I *had* managed, through some occult exercise of personal power, to make the therapeutic boundaries Dr. B guarded so zealously disappear, then of course I would have lost the means by which I obtained my once-a-week fix of unconditional positive regard. This was a familiar psychoanalytic paradox, a handy tool for dredging up the quandaries of infantile rage, and when I confessed my fantasy, Dr. B made just this use of it.

Dr. B's physical expressiveness was a gift, but sometimes it betrayed him. His face colored easily, and I could often see a look of eager anxiety spring into his eyes just as he was about to offer an interpretation. I liked him better silent than talking, because when he spoke he sometimes said the wrong thing, jarring me out of my meditations. His unquestioning acceptance of the tenets of his profession often angered me, and so did the way he turned my challenges back on me by engaging their emotive content rather than their substance.

I questioned him, for example, about payment. Dr. B charged the going rate, then eighty dollars an hour. Perhaps because he was the first therapist I hired myself, and because I've been generally slow to awaken to economic realities, the size of his fee came as a shock to me.

When I asked him to justify it, he offered the familiar Freudian explanation: The patient must pay enough to feel that he has a stake in his own analysis. I triumphantly pointed out to him—being married to a philosopher had sharpened my debating skills—that Blue Cross/Blue Shield paid most of the fee for my therapy. If he really believed in the Freudian rationale, he should refuse to accept third-party payments!

Here I had him, and he retreated. The next time the issue came up, he defended his fees by insisting that he was entitled to a "living wage." My response was to repeat this phrase and hoot at him. A living wage! He lived—I knew this because our town was small enough that people knew these things—in an architect-designed house overlooking the lake. He kept a large boat docked at the marina. I could see I had finally succeeded in making Dr. B angry; his face was blazing.

I went on to concede that of course he deserved to make a comfortable living. But was it really necessary to charge eighty dollars? How about thirty dollars, thirty-five dollars, something that a non-wealthy or uninsured person might be able to pay? Dr. B smiled slyly. Are you asking me to give you a break? he said. No, I insisted. I'm talking about a matter of principle. I'm talking about *all* your patients.

You're the only patient, said Dr. B. (This was an echo of a refrain I heard from him whenever I speculated about other patients or asked questions about them.) I was visited by an inspiration: Hah! I cried. I'm the only patient, am I? No *wonder* you charge so much!

That round went to me. Dr. B and I never discussed his fee again. When I raised the subject, or alluded to it obliquely, he crossed his arms over his chest and gave me a look I had come to know and loathe—a steady wide-eyed gaze qualified by a faint, enigmatic smile. I'm waiting patiently, that look said, for you to come off it.

After a time—a little less than a year, as I remember—the "transference phase" of my therapy with Dr. B ended. Quite suddenly, the vivid, stagy anger, the attraction, and the fantasies all evaporated, leaving me wondering how emotions that had seemed so intense could show themselves to be so shallow and evanescent— a shimmering film, an oil slick on a puddle.

The drying up of all the juicy feelings I had been enjoying in my therapy prompted me to reread "Lying on the Couch," one of Farber's late essays, written after his stroke. I looked it up in search of a passage in the last paragraph where Farber deplored the general acceptance of the notion of a "decibel scale" of emotion, "on which, intensity, significance and validity are all directly proportional, and increase as they climb the scale." Farber admitted to having felt the kinds of powerful emotions that register high on this scale—"as we all do"—but he took a characteristically detached attitude toward them: "[I]t is usually my inclination to endure rather than cherish them."

Reading Farber again—I hadn't in many years—brought back his quiet voice, his honesty, his wit, his delicate discriminations. In this piece, Farber expressed his doubts about the "revelatory mode" in psychotherapy, those moments of overwhelming emotion that, when subjected to analytic pressure, yield the "Aha!" reaction and a new, radically altered understanding of the past. Reading it then, when I was deep into a therapy that continually offered temptations of exactly the kind Farber anatomized, was a chastening experience. This was a moment when I came close to quitting therapy with Dr. B.

Farber described his experience of a revelatory moment during his training analysis. As he lay on the couch, he overheard the young son of his analyst practicing the violin in a nearby room, and by a chain of association—which he conscientiously verbalized—he retrieved a painful and humiliating childhood memory of succumbing to stage fright at a state violin contest (Farber was a passionate amateur violinist; the violin, Anne said, was his "voice.")

He also recalled that his father, instead of showing sympathy for his son's humiliation, "looked furious." Years later, remembering the anger on his father's face as he lay on the analyst's couch, Dr. Farber began to weep, and with his tears came the realization that his father's cruelty had altered the course of his life, discouraged him from pursuing a musical career.

For a while after he left his analyst's office, Dr. Farber took his epiphany to be a true illumination, but soon this compelling new vision of the past began to fade as Farber once again remembered the real nature of his relation to his father and to music.

> [T]here was never a dramatic parting of the ways between my father and me. Our life together was hectic, full of struggle and reconciliation, both rewarding and disagreeable, depending on forces I shall describe in my next novel. . . . [M]y musical talent was modest and I knew it. There was never a serious inclination—leaving my fantasies aside—to make music my profession.

The kind of revelatory "truth" Farber examined with such a jaundiced eye in this essay is different from another kind of truth he found more interesting, a truth "problematical, partial, modest—and still breathing." But he acknowledged that revelatory truth has a great allure: It seems to answer our craving for order and meaning. It gives our chaotic histories a satisfying "shapeliness." "Revelation," Farber wrote, "tends to have a certain loveliness of form that is quite unrelated to—and in fact may be quite in defiance of—what is revealed." The "essentially esthetic" satisfactions of revelatory truth are coarsening and potentially addictive, because they tend to dazzle us, to blind us to the fragmentary and elusive truths that Farber championed.

Farber took a further, harder look at the "revelatory binge" he indulged in on his analyst's couch:

> That performance was not merely uncharacteristic of me, it was alien and unnatural, it was inherently false, and I should have known it. Enthralled already by the ideology that permitted— indeed provoked—these novelties of self-expression, and too naive—or too cowardly—to heed my tiny intimations of doubt

about the authenticity of my behavior, I played out the drama of my willed self-deception to the hilt. Self-deception, but deliberate. Also known as lying.

Now that the transference phase of my therapy with Dr. B had ended, the "working" phase was beginning. It was time to cut out the flirting and the sparring and to apply ourselves to the work of therapy.

So we talked about my marriage, a matter of some urgency to me. Dr. B's approach was to act as an advocate, urging me to articulate my anger at my husband and to assert what he saw as fundamental rights. He threw into question all my efforts to accommodate my husband's needs: What about *yours?* was his refrain.

Of course I enjoyed being the innocent one, the hotly defended one, but the lawyerliness of Dr. B's approach disturbed me. I knew that if my husband were the patient, he would receive the same treatment—at least he would if Dr. B had determined this to be in his therapeutic interest. I was dismayed by Dr. B's lack of interest in the complex, nuanced picture of my marriage— of the whole "life world" I was struggling to present. Often I felt as if I had spent the better part of an hour constructing an elaborate imaginary house, trying always to balance a wing of self-justification with one of judicious self-criticism, only to watch Dr. B carelessly kick the thing over in his hunt for the hurt.

Dr. B's advocacy was gratifying, but it unnerved me deeply. I resisted what I viewed as Dr. B's invitation to consider myself victimized by my husband's abstraction, his (quite unexamined) sense of entitlement, and his tendency to criticize and blame. I was primed to feel defensive about my marriage because, like everyone else, I had for years been exposed to the narratives—coming from the culture at large—of women who had learned to put themselves first, who came into their own only after throwing off the shackles of oppressive marriages. I felt vulnerable to the feminist charge that only a sap or a ninny, a weakling afraid of solitude, would remain in a marriage as difficult as mine. And I felt vulnerable to an internal indictment as well, my guilty consciousness that I had pressured my husband to marry me in the first place, my fear that our marriage could never transcend its origins. My very defensiveness made me feel I was a prime candidate for a sudden and dramatic reversal, a radical internal flip—a revelation of exactly the kind Dr. Farber warned of in his essay.

When I voiced my suspicion that Dr. B disapproved of my marriage, that he was working to unseat me from it, he shook his head so emphatically that I was inclined to believe him. And indeed he had made some comments that supported his denial. Once, for example, he remarked that even at our angriest moments, my husband and I rarely lost connection, and that we were capable of an eye-to-eye honesty that most couples never achieve.

I began to see that Dr. B was indeed fanning the flames of my discontent, but not with an intent to destroy my marriage. He was acting as a physician, "treating" me in a way that had obvious medical parallels. By stirring up my anger at my husband, he was introducing the psychotherapeutic equivalent of a medicinal toxin, but doing so in a controlled environment where he could titrate the agent, monitor and manage its effects. I think he believed that his advocacy would spur me to assert myself, to push back against my husband and gain a more equitable measure of power in our marriage. Dr. B's intentions were good; this much I believe. But I also believe that his treatment was risky and intrusive, and it goes without saying that it was manipulative.

Dr. B's view of marriage was founded in a view of demands and rights; Dr. Farber's was covenantal and emphasized the claims that each partner made on the other. Dr. B sought to uncover power relations; Farber would have asked me to attend to my own responsibility to the marriage: An honest accounting might rescue it; on the other hand, it might dissolve it.

On the subject of my marriage, Dr. B and I were talking past each other. I had come into therapy asking the implicit question — is my marriage a good one? Dr. B understood me to be asking, "is it good for me?" I wanted to know the answer to that question, but I was really after something else — the answer to a question Dr. Farber and I might have addressed. I can only phrase it, awkwardly, as follows: Is my marriage part of the good? It should hardly have surprised me that from Dr. B I got psychological answers to philosophical questions.

I resisted Dr. B's advocacy with a depth of feeling that went beyond protectiveness of my marriage. I had come to develop an instinctive aversion to rancor, because to feel rancor was to feel self-pity, and I feared being caught up in its familiar dialectic. The more I struggled against it, the more touchingly valiant I appeared to myself, and the further I felt myself sucked back into a destructive self-cherishing. To Dr. B, my resistance to self-pity was simply a form of denial. To me, resistance was necessary; if I yielded, my efforts to construct a self would collapse and I would find myself falling back into a kind of watery Boschian hell, a bog where I would rot slowly in a solution of my own tears.

*   *   *

I was reluctant to talk about my childhood because I feared that on this subject Dr. B would prove to be more of an "'Aha!' hound" (Farber's phrase) than I could stand. But it was natural that the subject of my parents would arise, and once they were brought into consideration, it was inevitable that I would begin to feel and resist the pull of causal explanation.

When Dr. B solicited my childhood memories, my inclination was to talk about Williamstown, to run my retrospective eye over it, to dwell in those moments when memories hang in a clear suspension, to describe the landscapes and the layout of the town in intricate detail, to tell stories about people who seemed quite peripheral to the central dramas of my life. I can't accuse Dr. B of betraying boredom during these reminiscences; he listened attentively, smiled sympathetically, laughed at appropriate moments. But I sensed a tension behind his appreciation, a repeatedly squelched impulse to pounce analytically on my rambling discourses.

My imagination worked by moving away from the psychological center of my memories; I felt compelled to try to delineate an entire world by providing a descriptive or sociological or historical contextual frame and then backing away further and surrounding that frame with yet another frame. Dr. B's tendency was to move inward, focusing in tightly on the dynamics of my family. (To him, my history was composed of psychologically charged incidents; to me, it was made of impressions.) The undertow of this tension, this submerged dispute, was almost constant. Dr. B believed that the outward movement of my reconstruction of the past was a means by which I evaded and denied some reckoning. I believed that it was far more comprehensively truthful than the zeroing-in that he favored; by resisting the reductive and deindividualizing suction of psychoanalytic explanation, I was struggling to preserve my own reality.

One day when I was in the midst of musing about Williamstown, Dr. B said something that first amazed and then outraged me. He broke into my reverie with an apology, and then, sounding a little hesitant and tentative, he asked me if I thought it was possible that at some point during my childhood, my father had sexually abused me.

When I found that I could speak, I asked Dr. B what, in all that I had ever said about my childhood, provided evidence for this hypothesis. He threw up his hands in a characteristic conciliatory gesture. Nothing, he said. Nothing, really. It's just that there are some things about you that fit a kind of profile, and I thought I should ask. What profile, I asked. A woman, he said, somewhat overweight, marital problems, difficult adjustments—a cluster of vague symptoms.

Vague indeed. I had gone into therapy with Dr. B with an obscure, half-acknowledged hope that legitimate psychotherapy with a credentialed professional might provide me a paradoxical haven from the contaminations of pop psychology. I soon learned otherwise. I felt the breezes of trend blowing through Dr. B's office in the early days of my therapy, when he went through a "patient as consumer" phase. I had found that mildly annoying, but now I was appalled to see that he had apparently bought into the recovery movement's hysteria about child sexual abuse, just then at its peak. What could I expect next—a diagnosis of multiple personality syndrome? I assured myself that I would have made good on my frequently repeated threats to quit therapy if I had not been softened a little by Dr. B's abject and repeated apologies. But the fact was that by now Dr. B's eagerness to keep me had gotten through to me. I had passed the point when I could have brought myself to hurt him by leaving.

Finally he explained rather sheepishly that he had asked this question under the influence of a speaker he had heard at a recent conference, a woman who asserted that at least half of all women who enter psychotherapy were victims of childhood sexual abuse by their fathers. Yes, he acknowledged; he probably shouldn't have given credence to this claim, especially since the speaker had offered no documentation. His inquiry about sexual abuse was not helpful? Then he would make it disappear.

Very often, when Dr. B allowed me to be in the right, I went home and picked a fight with my husband. The contrast was too sharp to bear: If Dr. B showed me such consideration and allowed me such latitude, why couldn't my husband do the same? Why couldn't everyone?

I think of Dr. B as a *tinted* man, an updated and affectively colorized version of the psychoanalytic "gray man." Compared to my early, radically detached therapists, he was reasonably interactive, quick to move into relation with me, to establish a connection of sorts within the narrow boundaries that his fundamental psychoanalytic ortho-doxy imposed. (And he was rigid about these boundaries: Whenever we ran into each other outside the office, the next session was given over to an elaborate parsing of the event, a debriefing.)

He was frank about the uses of our "therapeutic alliance": Our relationship would serve as a kind of mock-up. Our work together would consist not only of shuffling through my past, but also of examining our own relationship for patterns and tendencies applic-able to my life.

What about his own patterns, I asked? Wouldn't they complicate things? I could trust him, he assured me, not to let his needs intrude, or if that was impossible, to inform me of their presence. This he did, sometimes rather oddly. When, for example, I spoke of my rape, he interrupted me and confessed that the issue made him very anxious, and that I should probably discount any reaction he offered.

Dr. B operated under the extraordinary constraint of keeping his humanity out of our relationship unless it served a therapeutic purpose. If some errant tendril worked loose and struggled past the therapeutic boundary, it was subject to examination and extirpation on the spot. But he was also quite free to stir up my feelings deliberately, to flirt, to manipulate, to do any and all of these things as long as they were justified by the realistic expectation that they would serve a therapeutic end. For my part, I was also severely limited. I was free, of course, to express anything, but the rules of the game did not allow me, like Dr. B, to manipulate without disclosure.

Therapeutic gerrymandering had shaped the territory of our relationship strangely. Between us we had it all covered, but the shared portion was nearly nonexistent. Everything was possible between us—everything, that is, but mutuality. It's not exactly accurate to say that I longed for that crucial element—I was too wary of Dr. B to really miss it much.

What I did feel was an intensification of my growing disgust at myself for having returned to therapy like the proverbial dog to his vomit, and for staying in therapy in spite of that disgust. After all, I knew better! I knew that whatever its ends, therapy was a sad, manipulative parody of authentic relation. But I also knew that in the outside world, therapeutic notions had become so omnipresent and pervasive as to be inescapable.

I returned to therapy for many reasons. My husband and I were suddenly fighting again, and our displeasure with each other had a familiar sulfurous smell. Our daughter was walking and talking, and the dreamy, abstracted term of earliest motherhood had expired, leaving me feeling stranded. I also felt that my relation to the future had undergone a subtle change—one that signaled, I can see in retrospect, the beginning of middle age. I found that I lacked, and had been lacking for longer than I wanted to admit, the unshakable confidence in my own sanity that I had once considered such an embarrassing encumbrance.

I returned for all these reasons, but also because therapy had been my element for so much of my life, and because in recent years it had become the place I had seen everyone else go. Perhaps my return can be better explained in sociological than psychological terms; I was herded back into therapy by a sense of panicky disconnection from a central social tradition.

By the time I became Dr. B's patient, therapy had overflowed its professional vessels, flooded the culture, and seeped into the groundwater. For years I had been backing away from this deluge, steadily climbing onto higher and more isolated ground, but by now the effort was beginning to seem quixotic. However I resisted it, every one of my interactions—as wife, daughter, sister, friend, and especially as mother—was subject to mediation by my own therapeutic notions and those of others. I was like an ex-smoker trapped in an unventilated designated smoking area, inhaling so many secondhand fumes that continued abstinence seemed pointless. I returned to therapy because, in a sense, I was already *in* therapy, but felt myself to be placed uncomfortably on its periphery rather than securely inside it. I went back into therapy because it had become the central institution, the hearth, of my society.

In the nine years since I left Dr. B's office, I've lived without therapy. I have a feeling, bordering on a conviction, that I've walked all the way through that house, and heard the door close behind me.

It's an odd sensation to be done with therapy, to believe it is no longer available to me as a recourse. I watch as people around me flow in and out of therapy, and as therapy flows in and out of them. I feel a familiar sense of alienation, and sometimes I'm also troubled by an obscure feeling of uncleanliness, as if my resolution to abjure therapy were a perverse abstention from universally accepted hygienic practices—as if I'd taken a vow never to wash again. Therapy is an ablution, a Ganges in which everyone bathes.

I've given up on therapy, but Dr. B is still at it, still keeping very long hours in the same building. I know this because when I've returned to the New England city where we both lived—my husband and daughter and I have moved across the country—I've always made a point of checking the parking lot where he keeps his car, and I've seen it there early and late.

Once I caught a glimpse of Dr. B himself, though he never saw me. I spotted him through the window of an expensive men's clothing store directly opposite his building, a place where I would never have set foot in the years I lived in this town, but where I found myself one weekday two Junes ago at ten minutes before twelve, browsing among the ascots and cummerbunds and looking out across the street toward Dr. B's building. He appeared at seven minutes to, and stood outside the door, taking the air during his abbreviated lunch hour. I noticed that he had removed his tie; his blue oxford-cloth shirt had worked loose from his belt, and it billowed around his chest as he stood in the dark rectangle of the doorway, stretching out the stiffness of a long, sedentary morning, massaging his lower back with his thumbs. For a moment he looked straight at me, but unseeingly, his eyes squeezed shut in an isometric grimace. After this brief, violent muscular contraction, he let his face relax, propped his back against the door, and watched the human traffic passing through the pedestrian mall, for all the world like a shop-keeper taking a break during a slack moment. He was observing a marketplace scene of the 1990s—roving packs of youths with neon pink and green buzz cuts, musical panhandlers, municipally sanctioned jugglers and clowns, hawkers of silver rings and tie-dyed halter tops, mothers and children waiting in line at the face-painting booth, shoppers weaving in and out of Victoria's Secret and The Gap.

Dr. B looked much the same, perhaps a bit balder. He looked a little weary too, but who wouldn't, after a morning spent attending to the back-to-back monologues of six patients? I could see that he was still slender, upright, and fit, good for many more years of practicing therapy.

8

BEYOND THERAPY

I arrived in Dr. B's office as a kind of psychoanalytic Trojan horse, with a bellyful of Farberian notions that were bound to subvert any conventional therapy. I often accused myself, as Dr. B inclined his ear to me, of undertaking this therapy in bad faith. But in Dr. B's office there was no way to voice this compunction. To him, any concern with bad faith was only a particularly complicated form of resistance.

I found it easy to sniff out Dr. B's worldview. Large sections of it were in place for me already, as they would have been for nearly any semieducated person living in the second half of the twentieth century. The parts of Dr. B's ideology were connected to one another in a far more orderly way then the noncontiguous pieces of Dr. Farber's unsystematic collection of beliefs, longings, and preoccupations. Anyone acquainted with a sampling of Dr. B's thinking could readily infer the rest.

Though Dr. B. never told me so, and never would have, I knew how deeply he must have disapproved of Farber's handling of my case. In Dr. B's view, Farber would have been responsible for any harm I might have incurred as a result of the illegal and dangerous medical procedure I underwent because he refused to authorize a therapeutic abortion. Dr. B would have called him to account for his cavalier and reckless baiting of my father at our meeting with my parents in Stockbridge, and for tacitly encouraging me to transfer my allegiance from my parents to him. Dr. B would certainly question Farber's failure to accurately assess my readiness to live independently in an environment like New York, and he would fault Farber for allowing me to cross the boundary of his private and family life—making friends with his wife, eating at his table, drinking with his friends, and caring for his children. He would point to my collapse into dependency as a lesson in the consequences of such trespassing. And he would condemn in the strongest terms Farber's violation of the injunction that a therapist must never allow his own unanalyzed emotions to contaminate the therapeutic environment. He would judge Farber's loss of control in the matter of Daniel's deception to be highly unprofessional, and all the more so because he was so obviously taking out on me his disappointed rage at another patient.

Assembling this imaginary bill of particulars has been an interesting exercise for me, because it brings into bold relief how radically Farber departed from the axioms of conventional psychotherapy—so far that I must say I find it a little disturbing that he stayed in the profession at all. Looking at this list, I can well understand how Dr. B—or any mainstream psychotherapist—would have no choice but to judge Farber guilty of serious malpractice.

And in fact Dr. B would have been right to say that much in my attachment to Dr. Farber was highly neurotic and self-damaging, and right to say that Farber's explosion was devastating to me. He would have been right to point out the undeniable connections between my early experience with my parents and the apparent failure of my therapy with Farber. He would have been right to observe that in my attachment to both Farbers I reenacted the losses I suffered in early childhood. In both cases my attempt to align myself with one parent or parental figure resulted in my loss of the other; in both cases I "fell between" the two.

He would have been right to say that I was harmed by Farber's explosion, and that its effects stayed with me for many years. I suppose he could have said, quite plausibly, that in those moments when I knelt on his carpet, weeping and begging, Dr. Farber became the very embodiment of my own harsh, primitive, and irrational superego.

And indeed, that hour remains encysted in my memory. I've returned to it year after year, examined it from every angle, and still it defies explication. I was galvanized by my first reading of Kafka's "The Judgment" because in this story I recognized the same atmosphere of uncanny heaviness that hung over that session, the sense that every word carried an extra, echoing beat. And I must say, though it seems a little extreme, that in my confession and abrupt withdrawal from Farber's office, I see something a little like Georg's suicidal dash for the river; I hear something like his cry as he lost his grip on the bridge railings: "Dear parents, I have always loved you, all the same."

For many years I stiffly resisted any criticism of Dr. Farber, defending him fiercely from myself and the anticipated assaults of others because I wished so passionately to preserve him in my mind. Dr. Farber's thinking did not lend itself to extraction and removal; it was not an outline, or a collection of dried or frozen maxims. His thought was intimately bound up with his life and his self. Even his essays are maddeningly difficult to summarize.

To preserve what Farber taught me, it was necessary to preserve him as well. I felt I was carrying a shallow bowl filled with precious liquid over rocky terrain, and that any spill would mean an irrevocable loss. What I feared acknowledging was not my own responsibility for what went wrong—I was always ready and relieved to do that—but Dr. Farber's. I can make sense of my own failure, but what sense can I make of his? In resisting Dr. B's invitation to revisionism, I've resigned myself to the acceptance of anomaly. But what middle-aged person can claim an interior free of knots and lesions?

I understand how frustrating it must have been to Dr. B that I refused to consider taking even one step down a path that would have led me to the master insight he had in view for me, the devastating and liberating realization that I had been ill-served and damaged by an "impaired physician," a "wounded healer." Dr. B circled me like a dog trying to upend a porcupine, nosing me cautiously in what looked to be vulnerable places, getting stuck with a quill or two in the process. I was adamant in my refusal to be flipped.

It was not only his unacknowledged rivalry with a psychoanalytic thinker far more distinguished than himself that motivated Dr. B. It was also his genuine and quite pure desire to do his job well. The repudiation of Farber was the "Aha!" that I refused to voice in Dr. B's office, and that refusal blocked what I feel sure he would have considered the royal road of my treatment. If I had said, "Aha!" Farber would have vaporized, and in his place my father would have stood, the harsh judge and secret nurturer. And he in turn would have vanished, to be replaced by my mother, the aboriginal depressed withholder, gazing out at me from the pre-Oedipal fastnesses of my infancy.

*   *   *

Having made some reluctant concessions, having acknowledged the ways in which Dr. B was right—or would have been, if I had allowed him to be—about Farber, my answer to him is the following: So what?

If Dr. Farber's aim had been solely or even principally a therapeutic one, the criticisms I've attributed to Dr. B would have been germane. What Dr. B never understood was that in the name of therapy, Farber was doing something quite different. His aim, as he described it in his essays, was quite specific and modest, but even so, it was a radical departure from the ordinary goal of therapy: He meant to offer hope to his patients through talk. This was not talk that centered, necessarily, around their problems—it was just the best and most honest talk that he and they were capable of. He meant to break the logic of despair, and his goal in doing so was not primarily a therapeutic one: "[The patient's] despairing certainty has been exposed to the real world of discourse," he wrote, "and proved false." Surely this release from despair also provided the patient with relief from the pain of despair, but for Farber, like Freud, symptom relief was a secondary purpose. In both cases, the aim was not so much to restore the patient's health as it was to free him from illusion. The difference was that in Freud's case the truth that remained when illusion had been stripped away was a darkly mechanistic one, whereas for Farber, although his worldview was tragic, truth was transcendent, and always held a possibility of hope. Like his mentor Martin Buber, Farber believed that "man as man can be redeemed."

Farber was reserved and sometimes dour; he carried an aura of deep melancholy. This was surely the basis for the reputation that Dr. B angered me by mentioning. But the irony is that unlike any therapist I encountered before I met him, Farber offered me a real affirmation. For me, his sadness and his toughness made all the more credible his message of hope and his vision of the possibility of living a good life.

If Farber had considered mutual talk his "method," he would not have been particularly unusual: Many a therapist has distinguished his practice from those of others by seizing upon some style or angle. There are Zen master therapists, who delight in unsettling and mystifying their patients. There are therapists who are programmatic in their brutal honesty, and therapists who pride themselves on their nonconfrontational tenderness. What was unique about Farber was that when he encouraged his patients to talk, he talked back—that is, he *really* talked back. It was his acceptance of the implications of mutuality that distinguished him.

I came to my early therapies as a child with two opposing characteristics, a strong native capacity for ardor—my "Organ of Veneration"—and an equally strong, and contrary, desire to tunnel under the surface, to discover the rules by which people and systems operated. My mother was the first object of this hidden kind of inquiry, and psychotherapy, to which my parents handed me over in puberty, was the second. For me there was a strong aesthetic shame associated with both these inclinations, a familiar and pervasive sense that I was emotionally incontinent and overwhelming, too much for my delicate, cool, fastidious mother to bear.

After a few years of ardent mystification on the couch, I began to realize that "underneath" psychotherapy, what is to be found is a process rather than a cache of wisdom. (There is, of course, a body of knowledge connected to therapy, but this is not therapy itself.) Therapy seeks to keep itself empty: For therapy, any fixed content is an obstruction that interrupts the process I've called "suction."

It was when I became Dr. G's patient in Washington, when I was allowed to sit up in a chair and look into the therapist's eyes, that I began to understand that there is no wisdom to be had from psychotherapy. And simultaneously, I fell into the error of succumbing to the familiar shame I attached to my investigative impulse. In a self-punishing inversion of ardor, I sought to put myself beyond rejection by making myself a purified, minimalized, grublike thing.

Imagine, then, the impact my first encounter with Farber had on me. I was like an underground burrower who has been digging for years and suddenly finds himself surfacing — into a cathedral.

What accounts for the sense of recognition I felt when I first encountered Dr. Farber at Riggs? From the first, his gravitas, his distinction, were so immediately and overwhelmingly apparent that even in my deteriorated and boredom-numbed condition I recognized them. It was as if another self continued to live inside the therapeutic self I had become, lying slack but fully jointed, waiting for some salutary yank to spring alive.

And spring alive I did. My best self was born in dialogue with Farber. During some of our talks, I was able to close the rift my therapeutic education had opened up in me, to own and acknowledge not only my vulnerability but also my contrarian energies, my desire for truth, my rude spiritual health. What remained problematical, of course, was the fate of that newly integrated self every time I left Farber's office. Like the patient he cites in his essay "Despair and the Life of Suicide," I turned in the doorway to ask with my eyes the question I knew better than to voice — "But haven't you something *useful* to say to me — something I can use after I leave here?"

Farber never wrote much about his own practice of psychotherapy. In an effort to trace the evolution of his clinical thinking, I've recently turned to Martin Buber, whose influence on Farber was enormous. I must confess I had never been a Buber enthusiast: I reacted allergically to the mysticism of *I and Thou* when I first read it—or tried and failed to read it. I preferred to receive Buber indirectly, mediated by Farber's sensibility: I found his intense spiritual sweetness more palatable when cut with Farber's acerbic worldliness.

But recently a knowledgeable friend directed me to essays in which I found a Buber more straightforward and less programmatically rapturous than the one I had known. One of these, "Elements of the Interhuman," struck me as the locus classicus for several of the most important notions that guided Farber's practice of therapy. In Buber's category of the "interhuman" I recognized the territory I stumbled upon in Dr. Farber's office at Riggs.

Buber's "I-Thou" relation applies to encounters between man and man, man and nature, and man and God. The interhuman is the narrower subcategory of the "life between person and person." It is distinct from the social or collective realm. The interhuman is an end, not a means. It has no utility; it is not the foundation on which society is built, and it can be inimical to society's purposes. What happens in the life between person and person can carry psychological and sociological meanings, of course, but these are incidental to the fact of meeting itself.

It is interesting to remember the ways in which Farber deliberately confounded my expectations. He led me away from the familiar ways of free association and self-involved silence by opening up side paths—as he did when he startled me by asking my opinion of Joanne Woodward, for example, or when he interrupted me to relate a story about his dentist's charming and homely assistant, whose hovering smile sustained him through the ordeal of root canal. When he cut off my monologues by saying, "I'm not inter-ested in that," what he was doing, of course, was reminding me of his presence in the room. He was nudging me toward the possibility of dialogue, demonstrating to me its proximity to our talk at every moment, even those that seemed too odd or humble to carry an emotional charge. The heart-lifting sense of return I felt was my recognition of this realm. It is one, after all, that every human being knows. Buber called it "the ever-near mystery": Its very familiarity disguises it.

To me and his other young patients at Riggs, Farber offered a therapy that was pedagogical as well as liberating. What he taught was not so much a collection of moral precepts and prohibi-tions—though he was never shy about recommending and cor-recting—as it was a demonstration, through talk, of how talk is to be treated not as a means to a therapeutic end but as the central source of moral meaning itself.

When I've described my therapy with Farber to friends, a com-mon reaction has been initial interest and approval—any kind of unorthodoxy has an immediate appeal—followed by slowly dawn-ing suspicion and doubt. What concerns these friends is always the issue of power and authority. How can it be right, they ask, for a therapist to impose his worldview on a patient? Doesn't that encourage the patient to develop a false self in order to gain the therapist's approval?

This reaction, nearly universal among my interlocutors, reflects the cultural ubiquity of an obsession with power relations. This is the great preoccupation of the age, and I often slip into thinking in these terms myself. Sometimes I find that it takes a deliberate wrenching of my perspective to return to an earlier vocabulary of thought. Were it not for the fact that I live on the fringes of academic life, where I can witness the ways in which those most engaged in the game of uncovering power relations exploit this ideology to establish power centers of their own—were it not for the sharp distaste this spectacle has occasioned in me—I might have long since have forgotten the lessons my experience in psychotherapy taught me, and passively fallen into these lines of thinking.

The nondirectiveness and nonjudgmentalism of Dr. B and other similarly conventional therapists might seem to allow patients a radical kind of freedom, something unavailable in the outside world, where the reality of other people continually limits one's liberty. But because Dr. B held himself responsible for his patients' well-being in the way a surgeon does, and because he was licensed by his training to use covert and manipulative methods, it was really only the illusion, or the sensation, of freedom that he offered them. Farber was unafraid of influencing his patients, but unlike Dr. B, he considered them responsible agents. For his Riggs patients particularly, this was an extraordinary and sometimes terrifying liberation. We were not only the damaged products of our histories; we were also the damaged products of the formative influence of psychotherapy, which inculcated in us the belief that we were the damaged products of our histories. It was a revolution in our thinking to understand that Dr. Farber considered himself to be responsible to us, not for us.

Buber wrote about "seeming"—the desire to control the impression one makes on the other. When this seeming masquerades as being, authentic dialogue becomes impossible. But interestingly, he allowed for the possibility of a kind of authentic "seeming" in those encounters—implicitly pedagogical—where legitimate authority is accepted and embraced: "where a lad, for instance, imitates his heroic model and while he is doing so is seized by the actuality of heroism, or a man plays the part of a destiny and conjures up authentic destiny."

In Buber's notion of "seeming" I recognize the damaging effects of my self-consciousness and my desire to burrow under the surface of my encounters with Farber to discover the hidden rules that regulated them. But in reading about the "authentic seeming" that Buber allowed in pedagogical relationships, I'm also, and poignantly, reminded of the hours I spent in Dr. Farber's chair at Riggs. I wonder now if I was unnecessarily harsh in my self-judgment, if the shame I felt about my idealization of Farber and my appropriation of his thinking was the source of the misunderstanding between us, and not the idealization itself. In his essay "The Therapeutic Despair," Farber observed that the "supposedly inauthentic stages" of recovery in which the imitative, idealizing patient becomes "a rag bag of oddly assorted scraps of theory, manner, and language, filched mainly from the therapist," are inevitable, and not, in fact, inauthentic at all. One of the therapist's duties, Farber remarked, is to help the patient recover from the therapy. This should have been the last lesson of my therapy with Farber, but because I bolted from his office, it went untaught.

The central irony of my life in therapy is that I did indeed develop a "false self". But my false self was exactly the product of my compliance with what I understood to be the rules of the highly orthodox psychoanalytic psychotherapy to which I was subjected in my adolescence. My true self had its beginnings not only in dialogue but also in imitation and idealization—in my ardent and unqualified acceptance of Dr. Farber's authority as my teacher and friend. To become ensnared in idolatry is an occupational hazard for every acolyte. My case has been an extreme one that only time, apparently, could remedy.

*   *   *

Buber took a grim view of modernity, and Dr. Farber—thoroughly modern though he was in many ways—tended, as he grew older, to share it. When Buber spoke of "an analytic, reductive, and deriving look between man and man" that was destructive of the possibility of mutuality and dialogue, he was referring to psychoanalysis, the science whose aim is "to contract the manifold person, who is nourished by the microcosmic richness of the possible, to some schematically surveyable and recurrent structures."

The dilemma was clear to Buber: "The perception of one's fellow man as a whole, as a unity, and as unique—even if his wholeness, unity and uniqueness are only partly developed, as is usually the case—is opposed in our time by almost everything that is commonly understood as specifically modern." Buber made this observation in the middle of the twentieth century. How interesting, and dismaying, it is to wonder how he—and Farber—would assess the progress of psychotherapy in the past twenty years. What would Buber, and Farber, have to say about the primacy of psychopharmacology, the widespread use of a new class of drugs that reach past manifest emotion into identity itself? (I remember Dr. Farber once remarking that he would prefer to lock a patient in his room than to prescribe a tranquilizer). How would they judge the phenomenon of the recovery movement—in some ways a direct outgrowth of psychotherapeutic ideology, in others a crude reaction against it—that sprang into full and ghastly bloom in the years after Farber's death? I find it unsettling to hear distorted echoes of Farber's thought in the recovery movement's familiar exhortation to let go of one's will.

None of this could have been predicted, I suppose, but neither would it have come as a surprise. It was clear when Buber was writing midcentury that a psychotherapeutic ethic was in ascendancy, and that for this ethic to prevail, more and more that was heretofore accepted as a part of the human condition, to be endured or celebrated or transcended through art or religion or unselfish love, would be relegated to the realm of the pathological. There were benefits in this, of course—no sensible person could deny that therapy practiced as an art can be a force for good—but in the general progress of therapy, there was also a great and terrible loss of meaning. It was the realm of the interhuman that steadily shrank as therapy advanced. The democratizing and leveling influence of the recovery movement only accelerated this process and widened therapy's scope. The world we live in now is one in which nearly all of us, whether enrolled formally in psychotherapy or not, are so thoroughly indoctrinated in the ideology of therapy that society has remade itself in therapy's image. To one degree or another, nearly every encounter looks like therapy now, and often it seems to me that human relations have devolved into something resembling a daisy chain of apes delousing one another. If therapy is all that we can give, or receive, then the possibility of mutuality has all but vanished. We have moved a step beyond T. S. Eliot's prophecy, which Farber used as an epigraph for his essay about despair and psychotherapy:

> *The whole earth is our hospital*
> *Endowed by the ruined millionaire,*
> *Wherein, if we do well, we shall*
> *Die of the absolute paternal care*
> *That will not leave us, but prevents us everywhere.*

*   *   *

I've struggled to make sense of Farber's angry explosion at me over the matter of Daniel's deception, arriving at the tentative hypothesis that he was beginning to be ill, and in his illness, had fallen into despair. Let me revise that, and observe that although it would be unbalanced of me not to allow the possibility of a medical factor in the darkening that seemed to overtake him, it would also be an unexamined capitulation to the spirit of the age to grant it too much weight. How easy and natural it is for me to think in medicalized terms, and what a handy weapon this kind of free-lance diagnosis makes for the discharge of anger. And there can be no doubt that I am angry at Dr. Farber for his behavior toward me that day.

But once again, let me in turn revise *that*: To put emphasis on my anger is itself a capitulation to the spirit of the age. Instead, let me say that I judge him to have acted wrongly and badly. His explosion was unkind, unfair, and self-indulgent. Under cover of his understandable exasperation at my neediness and dependency, he allowed himself to throw what amounted to a destructive tantrum.

His anger at Daniel was magnificent, the full and thunderous expression of his passion for honesty between friends, even—or especially—if the friend in question happened to be a patient. It was a confirmation of the very high standard to which he held this friend and this friendship, an expression, in its own way, of love. Perhaps it was a bit too magnificent; perhaps he had slipped into a state that he should have recognized as verging on what he would have called "pridefulness." Perhaps it was unstable and unsustainable, as all such essentially false and despairing states are. There was a palpable sense of defeat in his deflected rage, and also a sense that he was reacting to something more general than Daniel's particular deception—to some recently loosened force at large in the world.

Farber may have been ill, but he was still himself, still responsible, and it was a clear-sighted kind of despair that was beginning to undo him then—despair at the ravaged cultural landscape that the march of therapy had already left in its wake at the end of the 1960s, despair at living in a world where even the possibility of truthfulness had been called into question.

The years went by and every week I rode the elevator to Dr. B's office. I sat in his small, boxy, soundproofed waiting room, watching his silver sailboat mobile float and twirl in the air currents. Every week I leafed through one of six issues of *Smithsonian Magazine* and listened to the hushed burble of a PBS newsreader emanating from the sound system on the lowest shelf of a blond wooden cabinet. I trailed my finger along the surface of the soil of Dr. B's wandering jew and found it neither damp nor dry. And every week, a minute or two after the hour, Dr. B opened the double doors of his office and greeted me in exactly the same way. "Hel-looo, Emily," he called out softly, as if he were hailing me across a body of water.

Meanwhile, time was passing in the outside world. Fast-food and discount outlets were springing up on the outskirts of our small city. The formerly sleepy downtown was changing rapidly and radically; chic bars and boutiques and stores selling herbal remedies appeared, and pushcarts piled with loaves of sourdough bread. An underground mall was excavated, aboveground parking garages were erected, and the days when the escalator in J. C. Penney's had a statewide reputation as a point of interest passed away.

My husband finished one book and began another, far more ambitious one. I defended the master's thesis I had taken two years to write, and received my degree. I taught English at the local community college in borrowed high school classrooms that were kept so cold my students took notes wearing mittens. I joined a writing group composed of women who taught at the university and a few faculty wives; one of our number, a fiction writer, suddenly left her husband, published a novel that made her briefly famous, then lapsed back into obscurity. I quit smoking, took up running, resumed smoking and gave up running, quit smoking again, and took up walking. I began to find bands of white growing under the thatches of brown hair just above my ears. My daughter started school.

Things changed, but in New England academic life, most things change in a familiar, circularly recurrent way. Leaves turned, snow flew, mud dried, and lilacs bloomed. At the beginning of the fall semester, my husband and daughter and I drove to the cider mill and bought bags of early apples, which overturned in the trunk of the car and were sent rolling and rumbling like a battery of small tanks with every acceleration. The fall term continued through each year's desperately improvised Halloween costume and Thanksgiving in New Jersey with my husband's parents, and ended in the piles of bluebooks my husband carried home, just as my father had done, and the late-night special-pleading phone calls he took from students; winter ensued, days began before dawn with the flurry of getting ready for school and ended after dusk with simple suppers and early bedtimes. Mud season arrived, and we learned which marriages had not survived the winter. This was the time when the yearly crop of scandals were harvested—the geology professor recovering from gender-reassignment surgery, the harassment charges brought against the effusive Russian émigré in the theater department and later dropped, the suicide of a lonely, conscientious freshman girl.

And then the brief lovely spring came and went, followed by the lovely brief summer. The sight of my daughter, teetering on her bicycle along a narrow path through a meadow of high grass, brought back my childhood so vividly that I felt a sudden confusion of identity. This never lasted very long; I was always reminded of the difference between my daughter's childhood and my own—the ubiquity of television and popular culture.

The life I gave my daughter was never as beautiful or as rich with aesthetic satisfactions as the life my mother gave me. My daughter watched too much television, overheard (and pronounced) too many casual obscenities, observed too many fights, and was presented with too many store-bought birthday cakes. But still we managed to preserve some of the essentials of the faculty wife–faculty brat tradition, my daughter and I. We pressed autumn leaves between squares of waxed paper; we made batches of flour-salt-water modeling clay. We took walks together: In April we wandered into the woods behind the food service building and stumbled into a clearing where streams of white violets flooded through an opposing tide of silky young grass. In September we helped ourselves to handfuls of the Concord grapes that climbed over a chicken-wire fence along a windy promenade just above the campus.

In the middle years of my therapy with Dr. B, my life grew calm and stable. Whether this was a result of the therapy or my maturation or some other factor I don't know, but I do believe my weekly meetings with him had the effect of draining some of the anger and neediness that would have produced more conflict in my marriage. In this rather mechanical way, therapy served to keep my husband and me slightly separated for long enough to let the marriage heal. The heat of our early fights had been so intense that it scorched the ground of our marriage repeatedly. Any green shoot that tentatively sprouted in the intervals between our battles was blasted by the next one. It was in the Dr. B period that I began to see my marriage and family as a garden to cultivate.

Can't you ever be quiet? Dr. Farber asked me this question when I was describing a night I had spent with my roommates in Stockbridge, driving first from one bar to another and then from one party to another until dawn. The answer is no, I couldn't, not then. I remember youth as a kind of disease, a state of continuous agitation that made rest impossible. I've welcomed the quiet of middle age, not only because it allows me rest, but because quiet is a necessary condition for reflection, and reflection is the process of writing, at least the kind of writing I seem able to do. As I entered middle age, I began to feel the way a surgeon must feel when the anesthetic has finally had its effect on the patient: Now the anticipatory hovering is over, and he can finally get to work.

I began to appreciate routine, the useful way it rolls through days like a great adhesive ball, picking up and incorporating shreds of anomaly. I developed the changed attitude toward time that comes with middle age, the gratifying sense that I had learned the trick of riding its currents, gliding along lightly, anticipating the familiar sensations it brings, and letting them pass calmly because experience had assured me of the inevitability of their return. In middle age I began to appreciate time as an element; once I walked into Dr. B's office and exclaimed, "I am breathing time!"

I was grateful for my newfound equanimity and the well-regulated life that it made possible, but these things were not enough, by themselves, to sustain me. The steadier and more satisfying my life became, the more I was bothered by an obscure but persistent sense of suffocation, as if I were a swimmer urgently struggling up from an underwater depth, terrified that my lungs would burst before I broke the surface.

The years went by in such a regular progression that I find I can't remember what year it was when one day Dr. B was listening to me agonize about the difficulty of keeping myself from being swamped by the intensity of my husband's ambition and the vehemence of his anxiety. I ended my catalog of complaint by saying, "But he's a good person." Dr. B leaned forward and whispered, in audible italics, *"You've never said anything different!"* At this I burst into tears of gratitude. I was touched that Dr. B had been keeping track, and that he handed me back the raw data in such a generous spirit.

In retrospect, it seems to me that this incident marked an end of the struggle between Dr. B and me and the beginning of a real and constant, if very minimal, friendship. Human nature is such, after all, that given time and proximity, mutuality will take root in the least hospitable of environments. ("The essential thing," wrote Buber, "is not that the one makes the other his object, but the fact that he is not fully able to do so and the reason for his failure.")

I had always done the talking, but more and more now I began to do the interpreting too—in my own terms. My hand was on the tiller, and I was yawing wildly all over the lake in my maneuverable little sailboat, and it was fun. It occurs to me now that perhaps one of my many motives in my return to therapy was a desire to try my mettle against it, to seize control of therapy for my own purposes.

Dr. B invited me to talk, and I did, at length and with enthusiasm. My talking was mostly narrative and descriptive; when I spoke speculatively or analytically, I did so in general or philosophical terms. It was the kind of talk that had created tension in the office in earlier years. Even now Dr. B's eager-to-interpret look sometimes flashed momentarily across his face, but I could usually depend on him to stifle the impulse.

Although I failed to realize it at the time, what I had begun to do in Dr. B's office was to write aloud. I had written before, of course, even begun to call myself a writer, but my early attempts at novels and short stories were still self-conscious and derivative. My short fiction was ersatz *New Yorker*, and in my novels I was creating cat's-paw characters whose only purpose was to serve as mouthpieces for my opinions. I had not yet found my way out of the territory that Franz Kafka called the "shameful lowlands" of writing.

In the years since I left Dr. B's office, I've begun to write in earnest, and writing has allowed me—as nothing else, not even the wisdom of Dr. Farber, ever has or could—to escape the coils of therapy..I don't mean that writing has been therapeutic, though sometimes it has been. The writing I do now is the means by which I make sense of the world and my history. It is loosely associative, an exploration of the world through the self—very much like therapy, except the therapist is absent and I've given up all ambition to get well.

The compromise I had negotiated with Dr. B would have been impossible without the slender friendship we managed to develop, in spite of all the strictures the rules of therapy imposed on us. Now I could exercise my mind freely, subject to only the gentlest of pulls from the psychiatric suction machine—just enough to draw me out, not enough to swallow the products of my thinking—while Dr. B sat supportively and self-effacingly and steadily more invisibly by.

I followed the train of my thought, and recorded my struggles with the contradictions into which my thought led me. It was several years later that I found a written form that could accommodate the impulse to write aloud: This was the personal essay, and it allowed me to continue more formally what Phillip Lopate, essayist and curator of the genre, has called "basic research on the self." In the course of writing personal essays, I've come to realize that my objection to psychotherapy is not a resistance to introspection or self-examination—far from it! Instead, it is an instinctive bridling at an ideology that would appropriate and colonize my internal territories, mapping and charting them so that no more internal wilderness exists for me to explore.

Of course I must admit I can never sustain for very long a view of the world that is free of the influence of psychology. To pretend otherwise would be a lapse into faux-naive disingenuousness. For one thing, my interest in motive is inescapable, and it funnels me back inevitably into psychological explanation. But at least I can say that my ambivalence toward therapy keeps me alert to the possibility of those opportunities for "basic research" that fleetingly visit me, rare chances for a fresh and unmediated apprehension of the world.

Dr. B made writing aloud possible by relinquishing his therapeutic ambitions for me, and by giving up his rivalry with Farber. I'm grateful to him on both counts. Tempted as I am to say that when I was writing aloud in Dr. B's office I was addressing Dr. Farber, continuing the dialogue interrupted by our misunderstanding and his death, I must acknowledge this would be false. Dialogue requires two living partners.

So how can I account for my unshakable understanding that writing was the final realization of a process that began in Dr. Farber's office? Talking to Farber established a precedent in my mind for the legitimate expression of a private and subjective first-person voice—the essayistic voice, as opposed to the scientific or academic or scholarly one. It had to do with his licensing of the observer in me, the speculator. Quite typically, he undercut my grandiose overestimation of my own talent, but he also did me an incalculably valuable service by returning to me the inner life— he called it, in defiance of Freud, the "conscious life"—that I had allowed therapy to appropriate. This was chief among his gifts to me, another "time-released" reward that I fully appreciated only years after his death.

The kind of talking that I call "writing aloud" was nothing like the dialogic talking that went on in Dr. Farber's office—but true dialogue, after all, was out-of-bounds in Dr. B's. If my writing aloud were to be judged as talk, it would amount to a fairly pure example of the kind of monologue that Buber described as being addressed not to another human being but to a "fictitious court of appeal whose life consists of nothing but listening to [the speaker]." It was something other than talk, however, and thus—I like to think—it was exempted from the requirements of dialogue.

But neither was it therapy. Instead it was rather like a super-vised solitary game. I talked, Dr. B listened, and gradually, like the . Cheshire cat, he began to vaporize, leaving nothing behind but a glow of unconditional positive regard. He withdrew in a mandarin silence, allowing me a larger and lonelier arena with every session. In resisting his impulse to lure me back into the charted territory of psychoanalytic explanation, he granted me my wish to be released into the wilds of narrative.

Once, after five years of marriage, and six years before I became Dr. B's patient, I got so angry at my husband that I packed a bag and took a Greyhound bus to New York City. I moved in with an ex-roommate, found another job at Columbia, and made an appointment with Dr. Farber.

Dr. Farber had given up his office by then, and was seeing patients at the apartment. When I arrived, late in the afternoon, he shook my hand cordially and led me through the living room, past the familiar row of big dusty windows overlooking West End Avenue, and into the kitchen, where he fixed us both old-fashioneds. I stood at the counter and watched the assembly process, the slicing of the orange and lemon, which he carefully dotted with drops of bitters and sprinkled with sugar, the "muddling" with the back of a spoon, and the pouring of a jigger and a half of good bourbon into each sturdy glass.

We retired to Dr. Farber's study with our drinks in hand. When I asked Dr. Farber for permission to smoke—he had suffered his stroke a few years earlier, and had quit—he encouraged me to do so, and to blow the smoke his way. When I told him of my decision to leave my marriage, he nodded gravely. What he was conveying, it seemed to me, was not so much approval as an indication that he had gotten out of the approval business altogether.

Looking at him, I had the sudden impression that in the five years since I had last seen him, he had moved into old age. He looked wryer, more elfin, a little in need of a haircut. The essential strength and depth of his spirit were still present, but it seemed he had begun to conserve and protect himself. The *Sturm und Drang* of my life was only one of many clamorings, I felt sure, from which he had now begun, gently but implacably, to turn away.

When I asked Dr. Farber if he would take me on as a patient once again, he said no. We continued to talk for another half hour, reminiscing about Riggs and my New York days, and the tone of our talk was particularly warm and relaxed. At the end of our session, Dr. Farber walked me to the door of the apartment, waited with me until the elevator arrived, and shook my hand. I believe this was the last time I saw him. The next day I returned to my husband and our life together.

The last two years of my therapy with Dr. B were marked by a long wrangle about what he called the "termination process." We had not yet entered this phase, he cautioned, and so the end of therapy could not yet be envisioned. How far away in time was the beginning of the termination process from the end of the therapy? That varied, said Dr. B. How would we know when that process had begun? When the work of therapy had been completed.

But it seemed that under the terms of the therapeutic détente that had made my "writing aloud" possible, the work of therapy could never begin, and so, of course, it could never end. I could go on writing aloud, basking in the warmth of Dr. B's unconditional positive regard forever, or until my insurance ran out.

Real life intervened in the form of my husband's second sabbatical leave. Dr. B and I both accepted this as a stalemate breaker, and the termination process was compressed into a few summer months just before my family's yearlong removal to Princeton. During these last sessions, Dr. B often interrupted my monologues to introduce the theme of attachment and loss, but the stream of my thought continued to ripple along as it always had, picking up no traces of this effluent.

So it was a surprise to me when at the end of our last session, just as I was about to stand up, Dr. B, who since our initial handshake had never once touched me, rose from his orthopedic rocker and stood before me. In what took me a moment to realize was a clumsy, mistimed attempt at a hug, he grasped my head in his hands and pressed it against his stomach, hard enough that I could hear the gurgle of his digestion and feel his belt buckle bite into my cheek.

Never have I felt such a congestion of sensations; only in retrospect can I separate and order my reactions—first bewilderment, then a panicky vicarious embarrassment, then a flash of sexual arousal, quickly extinguished by my realization that Dr. B's embrace was an awkward eruption of affection and not a pass, then a suffusion of amusement and tenderness. I got to my feet and returned Dr. B's hug, planted a kiss on his cheek, and left the office.

ACKNOWLEDGMENTS

I want to thank my editor, Jo Ann Miller, for her help and patience; thanks also to her able assistant, Donya Levine. I'm grateful to my agent, Elyse Cheney, for her lively efforts on behalf of my work.

Thanks to Robert Boyers for his encouragement. I owe a special debt to Barbara Moore for setting me on the right path through the writings of Martin Buber. And thanks to Anne Farber for our renewed friendship, and for some memorable talks.

Thanks to Rosellen Brown for her inspired teaching. Thanks to Phillip Lopate for singlehandedly reviving the personal essay, and for the delight and example of his own work in the form.

Thanks to Richard Burgin, Ilse Hayden Winters, and Ann McCutchan, stalwart friends who listen indulgently to my boasts and complaints.

Thanks most of all to my husband, George Sher, for bringing his energy, his dogged persistence, and his marvelous intellectual acuity to bear on our mutual struggles with language and thought. Our continuing conversation is the medium in which my reflections live.

Renault
London
city.   bodyshop
Motability   0207
               2009016 .

Walnuts
01689 877787

Jenny B
07787171415

RAC
08007311173

RSA
0500474747

Motability
0207 6200400

TB66NK